COMMUNITY LIFE

What Is It, the Dire Need for It, and Why We Don't Have It

BARI MUHAMMED

PAGE PUBLISHING
Conneaut Lake, PA

First originally published by Page Publishing 2022

ISBN 978-1-6624-7219-0 (pbk)
ISBN 979-8-88654-968-3 (hc)
ISBN 978-1-6624-7220-6 (digital)

Printed in the United States of America

This book is dedicated to Imam Warith Deen Mohammed, who was and is the best leader a community could ask for, and to my sons, Abdul Hakim and Omar; my grandson, Omar; and my granddaughters Maryum, Malia, and Maysara.

I would like to also acknowledge Sister Jinaki Abdullah for assisting me in editing the book.

This book is also dedicated to my dear Sister, Baseemah Beyah from Masjid Muhammad in Washington, D.C. Sister Baseemah was the first sister to join me in representing the New Africa distributorship of CPC (Collective Purchasing Conference) in the Washington, D.C. area. She was always so supportive with the initiatives of W.D. Mohammed. She passed from this Reality (Life) around 2020. We will miss her persistence and sincerity. May Allah's Mercy be upon her.

"Community life, all the things that we need as a people to serve our purpose. We will call it the Four Birds taking flight, putting these concepts in motion:

- Culture
- Economics
- Education
- Government"

Bari Muhammed
Reference: The Wisdom of Imam W. Deen Mohammed

Al Fatiha
(The Opening)

With G-D's name, the Merciful Benefactor, the
    Merciful Redeemer
All Praise is due to G-D, the Guardian Evolver,
    Cherisher and Sustainer of all the Systems of
    Knowledge
The Merciful Benefactor, the Merciful Redeemer
Sole Judge on the Day of Religion
We worship You only, and we turn to You, begging
    assistance
Guide us on the straight way, the way of those on
    whom You bestow blessings
Not those who incur wrath, nor of those who go
    astray.

AMEEN

FREEDOM Is to Move

In our intellect to a greater vision, a
greater purpose. To a greater responsibility
until we are comfortable with ourselves in
our life and in our purpose on this earth.
Until that happens, we will continue to
be a burdened and confused people. "It's
a natural requirement for the life of every
human being that their intellect be liberated." (Imam WDM)

CONTENTS

FOREWORD

I am honored to be asked by Brother Bari Muhammed to write a foreword for his new book entitled *Community Life*. Like myself, he is a supporter and student of Imam W. Deen Mohammed (RAA) who, although left this world in 2008, is yet present with us through his supporters, his many words of guidance, and his initiatives designed to establish a model Islamic community in America that will provide what we need for our lives.

Prophet Muhammad is reported to have said that the best among you is those who bring the most benefit to the community (or to many others).

From the very inception of Al-Islam, the greater emphasis was placed on the importance of community life, a concept that was completely antithetical to the customary tribal life of the seventh century Arab people. They were the most divided people on earth and were deeply devoted to their tribalism. As such they fought to keep their tribal order intact by rejecting the prophet's message to bring them all into a unified community.

They persecuted the Prophet and his followers, eventually forcing them to leave their beloved Mecca and migrate to Yathrib, a city that became known as Medina.

Despite their opposition to the Qur'anic message of the Oneness of G-D, oneness of creation, and the oneness of humanity, after twenty-three years of struggle, the Prophet and his followers returned to Mecca victoriously and the whole Arabian Peninsula became a united people under the banner of Al-Islam.

To this day, the seat for this model Islamic community is at Medina, our example to emulate for all times. The people who were the most disunited in the world became the example of unity for all people seeking to establish a united community.

In Surah Ali Imran (3:103), Allah says, "You are the best community evolved or brought out for the good of all people, enjoining what is right, forbidding what is wrong, and believing in Allah."

We are much like the pre-Islamic Arabs because we are a disunited people. There is no debate to be had that the root cause of this disunity lies in the psychological effect of Chattel slavery.

We do not seem to be able to overcome the effects of this type of slavery to get up and do for ourselves what other people, who in many cases have just arrived, are doing for themselves in America.

It is a lingering problem because we are still dealing with the plantation ghost, which is in our subconscious minds, which stands in the way of us loving and trusting each other, working together, and uniting.

Many leaders, including the Honorable Elijah Muhammad, addressed the need for unity for African American people. They knew that the way to success was unity.

The Honorable Elijah Muhammad said we needed some of this earth that we can call our own in parts of this nation, which would allow us to separate from the white man. We now know that was part of his strategy to inspire us to establish ourselves as a strong, united, independent community in America.

Imam W. Deen Mohammed rejects the idea of separation. He contends that we have paid with our sweat and blood to earn our citizenship in America, and this idea was unrealistic and would not happen, and that we could build our "New Africa" model Islamic community in this country. Furthermore, he said we needed to claim our citizenship in America.

Among the many initiatives he introduced to us was the Collective Purchasing Conference (CPC). This concept was to buy quality goods from China and other places in the world and make them available to businesspeople in our Association of Muslims at prices way below their market value in this country to strengthen our community life.

The Imam, in one of his talks to us, said, "G-D created people to be a community and it is only in a community where you get your full freedom to live out your full capacity or your ability as a human being."

Dedicated individuals like Brother Bari Muhammed worked tirelessly to support all of Imam Mohammad initiatives. He traveled with the Imam from city to city and globally promoting and supporting the business initiatives of The Imam. His interest particularly was in the sale of suits purchased in China (called the China Initiative) at low cost. To promote the sale of these suits, Bari helped organize fashion shows, conventions and speaking engagements for the Imam to promote, display, and market these suits.

I am sure that his new book *Community Life* will contribute to helping us remember the work of Imam W.D. Mohammed who said, "Give me a good future." As his students and supporters, we owe him no less.

Khalil Abdullah Akbar

ACKNOWLEDGMENTS

I would like to thank Imam W. D. Mohammed (RAA) for clearing up our Mis-perception of G-D (one G-D, one creation, and one humanity) and our ultimate responsibility to G-D, our families, and the community of man (mind). And I thank G-D for giving me the opportunity to work with and for the ongoing phenomenon we call "community life."

I am grateful for the travel and the privilege of meeting and working with so many believers from around the country. Also, I would like to thank R. Muhammad for helping create the opportunity for me to work closely with our leader and all the other real workers who gave their all and all. You know who you are and who you're not. Finally, I was a single father with two boys part of the time that I was working for the Imam, so I thank my sons, Abdul Hakim and Omar, for being patient with me during the challenging times.

Bari Muhammed

AFTER DIFFICULTY

We want to make progress in the world.
We don't want to fail. The first step then
is to begin in your innocence. We want to
get to the end of the road. The end of the
road is not the end of living. The end of
the road is the end of the struggle, suffering and confusion. The end of the road is
a good life here on earth and hereafter; a
good life where you will feel good about
yourself. You will be able to feel good
about how you and your family are living.
You will be able to feel good about how
your neighborhood is striving and exist-
ing. Now how can you feel perfectly good
as long as there is another neighborhood
suffering like ours used to suffer, or there
is another nation suffering like ours used
to suffer? So you see G_D has created us
to be one family, to register the hurt of
all people, to feel their hurt and to not
be comfortable in our souls until everybody has a life that is livable. (W. Deen
Mohammed)

CHAPTER 1

Community Life = A Situation Where Responsibility, Opportunities and Benefits Merge, and Are Shared by Its Members

Remember/Think

"No big I's and little you's"
The Hon. E. Muhammad

Nearly from the start of his leadership, Imam W.D. Mohammed encouraged us to go into business with initiatives like:

- The honey bean supreme pie.
- Exploration of potential business possibilities with a cleaning products plant in Pennsylvania. We were assigned to meet in Baltimore for a few days of workshops on the products.
- Travel throughout the world to check on opportunities for the community.

- Development of the Collective Purchasing Conference (CPC)/Comtrust in Chicago for independent thinkers and workers. The independent thinkers and workers locate and purchase products and make arrangements with local businessmen and women to buy the products they need from a CPC/Comtrust distributor. As a result of these business ventures, a distribution route would be created for years to come. Yet a lack of serious support was injurious.
- Sought qualified individuals to handle the details of the operations of our business interests, yet there were no qualified takers.
- Introduction of shea butter and essential oils into the American market, but they were not developed or marketed properly. Now, look around. They are everywhere.
- Determination and persistence—Imam Mohammed never gave up. Once, we got a bad batch of shea butter from Africa, so Imam Mohammed built a processing operation in the same building as the Muslim Journal operation. But it didn't work; the shea butter was damaged too much.
- Investigation of car manufacturer in Indonesia, but the community was not ready for that big responsibility.
- Modest touch fashion shows are becoming popular around the world, but we are not in the network. Yet Graceline brand men suits and women

garments and fashion shows are an inspiration of
Imam Mohammed.
- New Africa marketplace.
- Coral calcium.
- Salaam nutrition.
- Silver jewelry.
- Purchase of halal meats from farmers in Arkansas
  involved Muslim American truckers moving the
  meat across the country, but there was no support
  for the idea. However, other Muslims capitalized
  on the opportunity, so we are still the number one
  consumer in the world.

Imam Mohammed created many opportunities for this
community to become economically independent; however, our *imams* and some business and community people
were slow to provide the support needed to bring about
success. This lack of support is indicative of the slave's
mentally which will not support leadership that looks like
himself or whom he feels he is superior to. The current
leadership must look at the track record and learn from it.
For there are no big I's and little you's, and those who think
like that, get in the way of real progress.

Nonetheless, Imam Mohammed is known for many
other accomplishments in our religious and social development:

- Women joined men in *masjid* assembly and worship
- Women placed in leadership roles in governing of
  masjid communities

- Worldwide respect for Imam Mohammed and our community by dignitaries and world leaders
- Provided a balanced exegesis of the Holy Qur'an which cleared up many misconceptions
- Honored as a Muslim world leader by many top Muslim leaders around the world
- Encouraged Muslims in his community to make *hajj* by escorting three hundred members of His community on this most sacred journey in 1977
- Motivated the New Africa mindset
- Scripturally revealed the schemes of Satan

Reflections on the passing and rising of W.D. Mohammed

The Creator says in the Holy Qur'an that He has granted the believer a manifest or clear victory. To realize this victory, all we have to do is believe in His words and accept His guidance.

We have to stop resisting responsibility and stop being selfish. We must roll up our sleeves and promote growth and progress through sustained work.

We also need to commit ourselves to following wise leadership and the "best traditions" from our history. I'm talking about leadership that knows how to navigate through the rough waters and difficult terrain we find ourselves in or we keep putting ourselves in. Leadership that has our best interest at heart—proven leadership.

Speaking of wise and proven leadership, we want to thank Allah for blessing this community, and the world in general, for the wise and methodical leadership of a man who will always be our leader—Imam W. Deen Mohammed (RAA). We thank G-D for blessing him with the courage and foresight in showing wisdom during the early days of this community's development.

He left us with many examples and efforts of work that is to be done and a clear vision of community success. All we have to do is stay humble and follow it. May G-D bless his soul and grant him paradise. And may G-D have mercy on us because we can be very hardheaded at times.

I hope that we understand by now that we should applaud Imam Mohammed for guiding us through those unsure times—for directing us closer toward real freedom, and we thank G-D for that experience with our leader and community. Now, we must realize our liberation and apply ourselves and stop looking for others to do for us what we should and can do for ourselves.

This brings me to the issue of freedom and economic dignity. Let's deal with freedom first. Imam W. Deen Mohammed says that,

"Freedom is to move in our intellect to a greater vision, to a greater purpose and a greater responsibility until we are comfortable with ourselves in our lives and in our purpose on this earth. Until that happens, we will continue to be a burdened and confused people. It's a natural requirement, the life of every human being, that their intellect be liberated."

Let's examine the definition of freedom in more detail. Freedom is to move. You can't be inactive and expect freedom. You have to be proactive and cause things to move.

Therefore, freedom has a lot to do with movement, the action on the part of those seeking freedom.

But where are we moving to or toward? Moving in our intellect to a greater vision means not being narrowly focused. It means seeing creation in a universal, holistic manner: one G-D, one humanity and destiny. And it means acknowledging your connection to G-D, humanity, and your destiny as a people.

A greater purpose implies thinking and acting with forethought and meaning in our lives by planning for the best results. While studying the best traditions of our ancestors here in America during the antebellum period, freed African Americans met annually to discuss their status as freed Africans in the United States of America. And to plan for a day when they could guarantee the freedom of all Africans in America and become full citizens. These great men—Frederick Douglass, Martin Delaney, and Henry Highland Garnet—realized that a Civil War was imminent and began training African American men to become soldiers so that they would be ready to join in the fight for their freedom. Their greater purpose was aligned with the principles of the US Constitution, and they referred to themselves as the Loyal League—in league with the US Constitution.

Freedom also implies moving into a greater responsibility until we are comfortable with ourselves in our lives and in our purpose on this planet. We should have begun "yesterday" to become more accountable for ourselves and our condition, for our families, and our communities. It is essential that we become less dependent on the system and more self-reliant, and stop looking to others to solve our problems, stop blaming others, and let G-D and His guidance improve our condition.

Sometimes, hard decisions must be made today so that tomorrow will be better (G-D willing). Until that happens, we will continue to be a burdened and confused people. Allah says that He will not change the condition of a people until they change what is in their hearts. This says until we make a lasting commitment to gain better control and accept more responsibility for our lives, we will remain a confused people with no common direction.

In conclusion, it's a natural requirement in the life of every human being that the intellect be liberated. So if the human being is to have life the way G-D (Glory to the Most High) intended it, which is to have the freedom and responsibility to grow closer and closer toward their destiny, to grow closer toward perfection; then his mind, heart, and soul must be liberated.

Allah says in his final revelation, the Holy Qur'an in chapter 16 verse 14:

> It is He who made the sea subject, that ye may eat thereof flesh that is fresh and tender, and that ye may extract therefrom ornaments to wear and thou seesth the ships therein that plough the waves, that ye may seek (thus) of the bounty of Allah and that ye may be grateful.

G-D has truly blessed the human being. All that we are required to do is be grateful and follow his guidance. If we exercise responsibility with this freedom that G-D is testing us with, we will, G-D willing, be successful.

Reflections on imam W.D. Mohammed
The imam's passing (we can't stop now)

Imam W. Deen Mohammed, leader of the largest indigenous Muslim community in the United States of American, passed from this world on Sunday, September 7, 2008, at his home in Calumet City, Illinois—a suburb of Chicago. Understandably, the passing of Imam Mohammed (RAA) was a loss to his community of believers, but we are reminded of a statement Abu Bakr (RAA) made when speaking to the faithful upon the passing of Prophet Muhammad (peace and blessings of Allah be upon him).

The believers behaved as if their world was coming apart, so Abu Bakr reminded the faithful, "O people whoever was worshipping Muhammad should know that Muhammad has died. Whoever was worshipping G-D should know that G-D is living and never dies." Then he recited the following verse:

> And Muhammad is but a Messenger. The Messengers before him passed away. Should you turn on your heels if he will die or be killed? And whoever turns on his heels will not harm G-D in the least. And G-D will reward the thankful. (3:144)

Imam Mohammed ascended to the leadership of the Nation of Islam, also known as the Lost Found or NOI, in February 1975. This was after the passing of the previous longtime leader and cofounder, The Honorable Elijah Muhammad. Imam Mohammed who was known to disagree at times with the philosophy of his father, The Honorable Elijah Muhammad (i.e., the perception of G-D, superiority of races, etc.), stepped into leadership and began to gradually move the community forward by correcting some philosophical points about man and his relationship with G-D. And he began to teach what real leadership is. He said that real leadership is being of service to your community, not your community being of service to you, like some of the leaders back then and presently think. Our community eventually became an integral part of the worldwide community of Al-Islam.

Besides working to improve his own community, the *Imam* began to develop relationships with other leaders and communities across the US and around the world. Through his efforts, he was eventually elected president of the World Conference of Religion and Peace. He was a pioneer and major advocate of interfaith dialog and cooperation among the Abrahamic faiths—Judaism, Christianity, and Al-Islam. He always thought the best way for groups and individuals to get to know and understand one another is through dialog, and he was right.

He was known for advocating and teaching his community and others how to read and interpret language so that we could get more meaning out of our studies. He taught us to take our thinking and ideas all the way to their logical conclusions. He was a very passionate man about his community members learning to think independently of the current trends of popular culture (blindly following trends).

During the last few years, the *Imam* recognized an urgent need for us to establish ourselves and to get back into business as a community. He advocated developing the twin giants in community life—business and education. Imam Mohammed was leading efforts and introducing business ideas and products to this community to, hopefully, ignite sustained business growth. He even sent business envoys overseas to places like China, Indonesia, Africa, and parts of the US to check out business opportunities. But these efforts could be no more successful than the sustained effort that we put forth.

Imam Mohammed was a man who was successful at demystifying religious concepts, thereby opening the heart and mind for a complete and rational relationship with G-D, our Creator, especially through an intelligent understanding of revelation. Our visionary leader, Imam W. Deen Mohammed, led and guided this community for more than thirty-three years. He did this successfully against great odds, such as lack of sustained, consistent, and strong support from many of us and a lack of sufficient financial resources.

The last time I heard the *Imam* speak at the convention, he said that, at times, over the years he and a few others would introduce a good business idea and product to the community. We would get excited. Start the work, let Satan distract, lose our momentum, and let the product or idea go! This attitude reminds one of the story of

Sisyphus and the rock—we get it almost to the top, and as soon as it's almost where we want it—at the top of the mountain—we let it roll back down on us. Let's respect the heights that Imam Mohammed was blessed to take us and not go backward.

Imam W. D. Mohammed taught us to focus on the project at hand and give it its due attention. Now is the time to do this and be consistent. Brothers and sisters, we don't want to be an embarrassment to our leadership and his legacy, so brothers and sisters, let's get our priorities straight and soon! Let us continue to support the ideas and relevant efforts that were in motion when our leader was here. While we are continually building on this great work, if we find that we are having problems with some people, we must find a way through the problem and if not, work around them.

Imam Mohammed worked with a lot of different people who didn't necessarily agree with him all of the time. He told me that some people will give you 60 to 70 percent, but you don't throw that away. You try to work with what you have. He says, "Use wisdom to get the task accomplished."

So now, more so than ever, let's stay in serious contact with each other. Let us prioritize our work and accomplish what Imam Mohammed left with us. Let us set the objectives and timetables like intelligent people do as we pursue our responsibilities.

In addition, let us do what our leader said in his final message: "Go back to our local communities and get strong and establish community life." We must stop waiting on the "big meeting" but come to the "big meeting" when we have something big to share. Also, do not fake a position or arbitrarily assign yourself any national duties. For you knew where you stood with Imam Mohammed before he passed. *Imams* or anybody else because you will not be appreciated or tolerated by the supporters of Imam Mohammed or other intelligent people. Moreover, we need to go to work in our local areas and get our ideas and products established in our local neighborhood. And like the Imam said, "Go back to your local community and get strong."

Finally, out of respect for our great and humble leader, who worked us through the psychological maze from slavery to freedom, we need to take his efforts to a new level and take this work to its logical conclusion—success. Please remember, no big I's and little you's.

Community life

We thank Allah always for the opportunity to exist, to serve, and participate in His marvelous creation. We thank G-D Almighty, the Creator of the heavens and earth, the sole judge on the day of judgement. The one who has no partner with Him in the rule of the heavens and the earth—He is G-D alone.

We witness that Muhammad the Prophet (peace and blessings of Allah be upon him) is his servant and his messenger and the seal of the prophets; the one spoken of in the Qur'an as being the liberator coming to purify the people and to bring them out of darkness, ignorance, corruption, and slavery into the light of G-D's truth. Praise be to G-D.

Religious expression requires a social context, i.e., schools, businesses, developed communities, and etc. Allah instructs us in the Qur'an:

> Rather, seek the reward of the Hereafter with all the means that He has made available to you, (that means with all the resources at your disposal), but don't neglect your share of responsibility in this world.

Everybody is obligated to some degree to be responsible.

"He brought the light" and everything began to change

Imam W. Deen Mohammed brought his followers a true understanding of religion and gave them the following insights:

1. Jesus being promoted and presented as a false Caucasian image of G-D in religious literature. This indirectly promotes racism.
2. Spiritual renewal—he took the baby language out of scripture and taught us that the metaphors and allegories (stories in scripture) had deeper meaning and that we should look for that deeper meaning.
3. He brought back the concept of community life.
4. And he taught us that the real life was the spiritual life, the life within.

5. He influenced the human being to focus more on the Creator (G-D).

6. He encouraged us to study our environment more seriously, and that everything has a lesson. He stressed that we should pay more attention to and follow the themes in movies.

7. He taught about holidays and how knowing the real meaning behind them benefits the mind. Additionally, knowing the motivations and reasons connected with certain themes free the mind and guide us toward truth.

8. By focusing on the African American experience and having respect and honor for ourselves, that brings more dignity to us as human beings within the family of humanity.

9. Most importantly, it may sound simplistic, but he taught us to think more seriously and carefully about life as Muslim Americans, having responsibility as *khalifah* or leaders and to take knowledge and reason to their logical conclusion.

"THINK"…for thinking benefits "Man."

CHAPTER 2

A Moral Summit

Wisdom and "Guidance of Our Special Leaders"

The Evil One threatens you with poverty
and bids you to conduct unseemly. Allah
promises you His forgiveness and bounties, and Allah cares for all and He knows
all things. (Qur'an 2:268)
The tree is known by the fruit it bears.
(Luke 6:44)

Prophet Muhammed (PBUH) said, "The Muslim, when-
ever he endeavors to do anything, he seeks to perfect it."
Unity: "A home divided against itself cannot stand."
Proverbs 603:37
John F. Kennedy: "Economic growth without social progress lets the great majority of the people remain in poverty while a privileged few reap the benefits of rising
abundance."

Cautious, careful people, always casting about to preserve their reputation and social standing. Never can bring about reform. We need to develop leadership with strong conscience.

W.E.B. Dubois: "Herein lies the tragedy of the age: not that men are poor… Not that men are wicked… Not that men are ignorant. Nay, but men know so little of men." (Ignorance can lead to all kinds of misperceptions).

Hon. Elijah Mohammed: "I came here to clean you up. The one that comes after me will teach you your religion." A character builder who gave focus on our community and economic responsibility.

Imam W. Deen Mohammed: One of the important things that the *Imam* taught us was *Deen,* our religion.

- He also emphasized for us to think. For thinking benefits. Don't be afraid to think.
- That our priorities are to develop schools, businesses, and community life.
- Citizenship. Be responsible for our freedom space because it gives one a sense of ownership.
- Freedom is the reward for hard work.
- "Most leaders today are not talking about values and citizenship responsibilities."
- "Allah made us to be one spirit, the spirit of Adam." Allah said, "When I have breathed into him of My Spirit, then you make *sajda* to him." That means, when we are in the spirit that G-D wants us in, his angels are at our service. Their existence is to support our life. They will support us in all of our endeavors.

1. Dr. M.L. King, Jr. said, "A day will come when man will not be judged by the color of his skin, but the content of his character." He pushed for social and economic dignity. The most dangerous criminal may be the man gifted with reason but with no words.

Reaching the summit

The Creator of the heavens and earth and everything in between, G-D says, "There is not a leaf that falls that He doesn't have knowledge of or is aware of that action." So never think you're doing something that He is not aware of. Whatever it is, always seek His grace and forgiveness because He is the most merciful, the forgiving (just don't keep doing the same negative or immoral thing over and over because His wrath is also at the ready).

What is this concept, a moral summit? I think it is when we strive to reach a plateau of behavior that was exemplified in the strong characteristics of our leaders and prophets, especially the Seal of the Prophets, Prophet Mohammed of 1,400-plus years ago.

I also think that this "call to action," this so-called moral summit must include the type of thinking that represents the total human being (his or her moral life, social life, business life, family and community life). None of these should be neglected as we are developing ourselves and our community life. One stumbling block that I noticed was this big elephant in the room that nobody wants to talk about—deteriorating moral problems in our society, no economic representation in the African American to speak of, slow planning and execution, and selfish superficial relationships.

A moral summit is what we are striving for, and I think we will get there. But out there, in great parts of our society, there is an immoral summit in full swing. Every man for himself, high divorce rate, homosexuality has affected a lot of our families, disrespectful behavior, and just plain hate. And we are trying to ignore it—that big elephant in the room.

There is hope, but how do we get there? This is a call to follow the directions and advice of leaders like Imam W. Deen Mohammed, who led us to the spring of moral certitude. But we have to drink. It is necessary that we develop community life, wherein we are self-supporting. Develop as a unit in our businesses and schools, and learn this religion through following his wisdom for us, given our unique position in this society (up from slavery and no establishment).

Remember what Imam W.D. Mohammed says: "Religious expression requires a social context." You can't just have Islamic life in your heart and in your spirit, and this concept applies to all faiths. Islamic life has to be expressed in Islamic structures: halal businesses, homes owned by Muslims, factories owned by Muslims, productive land owned by Muslims, hospitals, schools, transportation, cars, buses, and trucks owned by Muslims. With that said, let me also say that we have a moral obligation to establish business and community life in our neighborhoods.

Allah instructs us in the Qur'an to "seek the Hereafter with all the means that I have availed you." That means with all the resources at your disposal, "but don't neglect your share of responsibility in this material world." We want our developing leaders and ourselves to reach great heights, but we must stay morally based, no matter what good avenues we are working in.

As our developing leaders and ourselves begin to establish community and a viable business presence in our neighborhoods, we want to be situated where:

1. Our businesses are in close proximity to one another.
2. We live and work in those neighborhoods.
3. We are constantly strengthening our businesses by shopping there first, if possible, and
4. We encourage group ownership of our businesses, not just individual ownership.

With group ownership, you get more potential support from our community and properly generate more income. Also, there is less investment from individuals, and we have more sharing, caring, and concern, and the community feels responsible for keeping the businesses growing. On the other hand, if we only have individual ownership, there are more out-of-pocket expenses. The individual owner has less time to market his business, and that person is solely responsible for making sure everything is up and running daily.

It is imperative that our developing leaders focus on community life. It will give us more control and support for our cultural growth and expression. We will have more influence in the activities of our children's lives. It affords us better protection for our families from the ravages of the streets and media, and we can feel relatively safe and secure. It is where we can raise wholesome leaders. It also creates a growing perception in the community's mindset that the group is more important than the individual.

This is what our leader encouraged often. He would say, "Community life is what we must work for and accomplish." Equally important, Hon. Elijah Muhammed used to stress, "No big I's and little you's." But some of us were hardheaded, and that is exactly what we created; somebody is always standing over us.

Islam views business and work as a mechanism for attaining social justice, material freedom from slavery and poverty, and ultimately, as a means of accessing a gate of paradise. The Prophet (peace be upon him) says, "The honest merchant is with the Prophet."

That is how important it is. Imam W. Deen Mohammed makes it clear that Allah, the owner and maker of all things, material and non-material, in heaven and earth; intended that men engage in big business. But men had to purify their motives. "The worst pig," Imam Mohammed says, "is not the pig forbidden to be eaten by Mosaic, Christian, and Islamic Laws, but the pig in man's blinded spirit." Islam provides the balance between both monkish-ness and materialism.

In conclusion, to reach for the moral summit, we have a moral responsibility in every sphere that we are in. We are going to have to answer to G-D on judgment day as an individual and as a community, and as we know, judgement day starts now.

CHAPTER 3

A Moral and Ethical Redirect

Morals: following the decent path, conducting yourself in a manner that brings honor and respect to you as a human being (the crown of creation) and your community.

Summit: the highest point of a climb—the top.

How do we, as a people, correct our own behavior to get back on the side of G-D? Because right now, we're getting our behinds spanked by nature and by our own behavior. G-D sends us messages and warnings at times. So we have to be humble and smart enough to take heed. And it seems as though G-D has commanded nature to whip us into shape—to remind us that we don't control everything. And if we can't see this, then we are blind...or just stubborn.

Fortunately, not all of us are doing bad and immoral things, but the residual effects are a stark reminder of what happens when we keep ignoring the guidance of G-D. Periodically, we need to question ourselves, to gauge whether we are on the right track or not. Am I doing the best that I can do for myself, my family, and my community? Am I contributing something for the betterment of society? How do we check the negative influences in society? What ways can all the players in our community contribute to a more productive group life? Let's all make a lifelong consistent commitment to do this for the sake and health of our children and our society because our very lives depend on the right decisions we make as a people. We are talking about community life.

We must impregnate the ideas of community life and business development into the hearts and minds of our young people. This is a goal that must be achieved if we are to establish ourselves among other self-sustaining, progressive communities in society.

Business concepts and practices have existed all the way back to the great gold caravan of Mansa Musa, the eminent Muslim leader of Mali and builder of the Great Mosque of Timbuktu. He organized some of the largest trade caravans in the known world at that time. He demonstrated the importance of free trade by traveling long distances and dealing in a multitude of goods, such as gold, silver, ivory, incense, spices, oils, etc. He carried what was needed and wanted by those he traded with, and he brought back what his people needed.

So we must teach our children the dynamics and benefits of doing business with ourselves and others. We have to teach how important these business relationships can become and the good things that they can lead to in other parts of our lives, like cultural knowledge, cultural change, wealth building, and renewed respect among other business communities.

You may ask, why should we teach our children the importance of business principles and practices? The main reason is there has been a sort of "cultural disconnect" in our past and present community life. At certain points in our development, we allowed bad influences to come into our communities and misdirect us or take us off mission. And as a result, we have not been able to sustain respectable social, economic community life in this country.

As we were blessed to come through and out of slavery, we had aspirations and hope for a better tomorrow. We knew that we had to refine and sharpen our skills and attitudes. We had to reeducate ourselves for an independent go at life because we had been locked down and told what to do and what not to do all our lives. We were told where to go, how long to stay, who to establish relationships with, what to eat, etc. This submission to another people impacted our lives to the point that we were always looking out for the interest of someone else instead of our own. Their well-being and survival "trumped" our own. Their welfare and interests were more important than our own. For centuries this went on—all the way to this present day.

Consequently, this period of reorientation or reconstruction in preparing ourselves for a better existence started off and focused on what we had to do to uplift ourselves. People like Booker T. Washington, W.E.B. Dubois, and Frederick Douglas became strong advocates for our cause. Schools were built, and common values were adhered to, so we began to look and act like a developing people. Black

Wall Street in Tulsa, Oklahoma, and other economic efforts began to spring up across the nation. Our people were seeing and hearing about these community building efforts, and they were inspired from those examples of success.

Then, certain segments of the white population became envious of our achievements, afraid of our potential and afraid that our achievements would dispel the lies that they had been telling the world. Lies about blacks being subhuman and that we were lazy and shiftless.

This false perception began to unravel before them and their children's very eyes. So Jim Crow laws and other restrictions became the norm.

Yet this didn't stop the valiant efforts of our people to develop their own townships and communities. These townships and communities had all the necessary ingredients of an established society. Some of them had banks, lawyers, doctors, insurance companies, stables, repair shops, and schools. These were African Americans being of support and service to other African Americans.

The intense hatred and jealousy that I spoke of earlier turned into a campaign of false accusations. And the result was outright pillage and murder in some of these centers of community and economic activity. Black Wall Street in the Greenwood Community of Tulsa, Oklahoma, was burned down because of an accusation that a white woman was sexually assaulted by a black man. And this accusation was justification to tear down the black business community, the homes, and destroy the lives of many.

Ida B. Wells in a Red Record recorded that many of the lynching in the United States were not ostensibly due to the accusations of black men raping white women but were out of animus toward successful and independent thinking African Americans or toward men who had prohibited sex with consenting white women and were caught.

Ida B. Wells reported an incident in which the governor of SC turned an accused black man over to a mob:

> John Peterson, near Denmark, SC, was suspected of rape, but escaped, went to Columbia, and placed himself under Gov. Tillman's protection, declaring he too could prove an alibi by white witnesses. A white reporter hearing his declaration volunteered to find these witnesses and telegraphed the governor that he would be in Columbia with them on Monday. In the meantime, the mob at Denmark, learning Peterson's whereabouts, went to the governor and demanded the prisoner.
>
> Gov. Tillman, who had during his canvass for reelection the year before declared that he would lead a mob to lynch a Negro that assaulted a white woman, gave Peterson up to the mob. He was taken back to Denmark, and the white girl in the case as [sic] positively declared that he was not the man. But the verdict of the mob was that "the crime had been committed and somebody had to hang for it, and if he, Peterson, was not guilty of that he was of some other

crime," and he was hung, and his body rid-
dled with 1,000 bullets. (Wells, Ida. "History
of some cases of rape." The Red Record,
1895, The Project Gutenberg Ebook.)

Wells referred to these attacks upon black men and
justice as "lynching bees." During the lynching and burn-
ing of these men, Whites would take souvenirs of the event.
Bringing their children to see a human being murdered and
the body burned. Adults would cut off body parts or keep
pieces of the rope that was used to hang the accused.

During this time period, Jim Crow laws were in full
bloom. These laws and lynching were designed to keep
blacks in their so-called place. From these efforts to keep
blacks in their place arose the big lie of the myth of the
black rapist. According to the article "Race, Racism, and
the Myth of the Black Rapist:"

Before lynching could be consolidated as a
popularly accepted institution, however, its
savagery and its horrors had to be convinc-
ingly justified. These were the circumstances
which spawned the myth of the Black rapist—for the rape charge turned out to be the
most powerful of several attempts to justify
the lynching of Black people. The institution of lynching, in turn, complemented by
the continued rape of Black women, became
an essential ingredient of the postwar strategy of racist terror. In this way the brutal

exploitation of Black labor was guaranteed. And after the betrayal of Reconstruction, the political domination of the Black people was assured. ("Race, Racism and the myth of the Black Rapist" https://analepsis.files. wordpress.com/2019/10/mythbrch11.pdf)

Moreover, blacks could not eat, drink, or use the bathroom in the same facilities as whites. Society was solidifying its false claim that blacks were inferior to whites and didn't deserve the same rights and respect as the white man. Undoubtedly, this type of response from whites had a negative impact on the spirit of black folks, so many black people grew weary of the Jim Crow laws, which oppressed them and chose to remove themselves from the environment. As time went on and more civil right laws were passed and enforced, blacks began to use their newly acquired skills and education to take advantage of these new opportunities.

Our ancestors had a natural striving for community life—something that they could call their own and create from their own hands and their own minds. Our ancestors had good leadership, like Frederick Douglass and Booker T. Washington, that encouraged moral rectitude, common sense, and remembrance of G-D.

The dilemma

Imam Mohammed in a lecture titled "How can African American People solve their Economic Dilemma?

The Solution," he asks, "Why can't the African American people establish themselves? Why can't the African-Caribbean people establish themselves? We are all the same people from the same ancestry, and we all depend upon the white man for hope. We have no vision of our own. We're just following the white man's light; therefore, we stay in the dark."

Imam Mohammed continues, "The thing that is wrong with the African American people and their descendants is in following a people who are not responsible for establishing them in the world. If they would stop following another people and try to find G-D, try to solve their problems on their own strength, their own sensitivity, their own motivations, they would come to life once again. That is the answer, and it is as simple as that."

Imam Mohammed emphasizes that in our search for establishment, economically and socially, we must have integrity to question our own behavior as we have questioned the behavior of white people and follow the direction that our questions reveal. Equally important, he states that during our quest for integration, we failed to "look at the original creation and try to envision or determine the content of the life that G-D intended for us." Instead of integrating into a society that did not want us, Imam Mohammed explains, "We should have asked, 'What is in that content as direction for me living my life?'"

Clearly, in 2021, it is time that we make an exodus from the "white man," for the responsibility of making the world and society better has been passed onto us, the

Muslim or New African. G-D challenges us in the Holy Qur'an, "Let there arise out of you a band of people inviting to all that is good, enjoining what is right and forbidding what is wrong: they are the ones to attain felicity."

"The Solution"…respect, support, and
cooperation among good people.

CHAPTER 4

Seven Deadly Sins (The Road Blocks)

As we pursue happiness in life, beware of
the traps (sins).

—Embrace the Cardinal Virtues

Seven deadly sins plus one are a hindrance to community
growth and development (life). Consider this: "To flee vice
is the beginning of virtue" (Horace).

It is one thing to ignore, for a time, stories that you
do not understand or cannot relate to for various reasons.
However, it is quite another to ignore clear and direct guidance from scripture, from whichever book: BIBLE, TORAH,
QUR'AN, and from great minds.

The Qur'an says, He (G-D) also revealed wisdom
and guidance in a basic or fundamental manner (clear).
Moreover, G-D said his guidance would come in the form
of stories and allegories, which means if you are constant
and patient, you will be blessed with the meaning of these
stories one day, so be patient and humble.

Clarity will come to you, and you will be able to figure out the riddles and mysticism of life, G-D willing. In the meantime, work with what you know and understand. If we apply basic principles that we understand to the problems we encounter, we will be much further down the road toward success in our lives. As a priority, we need to first understand and apply that which is clear and fundamental guidance. I think that the closer we stick to common sense and wait on wisdom, then we will get closer to our goal (community life) without stumbling. Furthermore, we must always make sure we are a principled people. That is a people who value morals and ethics because if not, we will always be the victims of Satan's handiwork.

This way we are sure (G-D willing) to understand and avoid the following seven deadly sins plus one. All of this can have a destructive effect on any effort we make to advance our agenda. So those of us working toward community life must be aware of the following major distractions. The first one is lust.

Lust

Lust is the handing over of control of the mind and body to illicit cravings. This type of desire takes our minds off what is real and important. It also distracts us from the serious job of staying focused and goal setting. Lust is a poor weakness that whispers things compared with the richness and energy of desire, which will arise when lust has been put to rest (under control). So having a legitimate desire is a stark contrast from lust. However, it is all right compared to the extreme desire of lusting after something or someone. Lust is similar to transitory pleasures and imaginary comforts, whereas the real (balanced) desire is about genuine joy and a rich and strong identity.

Sex

Sex is designed to do much more than gratify mutual desires and fantasies; its life function is one of process. It is a tool for building community and for socializing individuals into persons. That is, human beings with multiple qualities who are connected to the fabric of society. However, when lust is a constant in our lives, it takes us away from "the balance" in life. We can become obsessed with sex; thus, sex becomes the focus. We all have desires, and we will never be free of them. They are designed for our good, and they are only burdensome when we seek to fulfill them with things that cannot satisfy our desires. The choice is ours. Will we desire the lasting or the transient? Freedom or bondage? Lust only offers an illusion

G-D offers the only reality. Our desires can keep us pinned to illusions, or they can redirect us to what is real. We have to learn how to deny ourselves and benefit from what is real and lasting, "a balanced life." We have to learn not to go to one extreme or the other. We must know when to say no or when to say yes. Lessons like this will help us control our growth and sustain a quality community.

Lust can lead to a life of hell. A life decaying until nothing remains. If we fall for the fleeting influence of lust, we cannot blame G-D for the results. We can only blame ourselves. G-D creates neither sin nor evil nor hell. They exist as the absence of what ought to be. Sin encourages us to create a world of our own selfish making. Therefore, hell is above all an absence of reality. In addition, lust is just a frame of mind that is smothered by a furnace of unrealistic fantasies that one constantly pursues.

Wrath

Wrath is the next of the sins we want to discuss. Wrath is anger, rage, extreme retaliation, or massive, disproportionate retaliation. Wrath is the love for justice perverted into bitterness, revenge, and violence. Therefore, we should become more aware of it and avoid it at all costs. G-D's wrath is the only righteous wrath and justified punishment for our continuous bad and disobedient behavior.

When our longing for justice turns to violence and scorn, we no longer share G-D's perspective. We move from being part of the solution to becoming part of the problem. We move toward wrath, another facet of sin at work in our world. Consequently, as we are building community consciousness, we should never allow ourselves to become self-righteous and bigheaded. We will not ignore group consciousness on matters concerning community for individual dictates.

If we are ever the arbitrator in a situation to make peace, we will feel the pain of one of the fighting parties. We will have to surrender our own potential rage if we are to help bring justice and fairness to the situation. We must learn and teach, that to forgive early on is one of the best acts we can do if we are to reflect G-D's will.

We must also care for the unity of our estranged brothers and sisters while at the same time, despising what separates us and them. And in the end, do all we can to mend fences. Be the peacemaker; one who would be a servant of G-D. One who disposes of wrath in order to reconcile the divide. Hence, in order for us to reflect the will of G-D, we must reject "wrath."

Hadith says, "Do not become angry." Often, you and I are most angry. Not when we have been hurt but when someone has hurt those we care about. Wrath plays on our inability to forgive. Our inability to deal with injustice with intelligence. Wrath is nothing more than hitting back. Ultimately, wrath is a deadly sin because it separates us from those we ought to embrace and cherish as fellow servants of G-D. So those of us who want community life and peace in our neighborhoods, we are going to have to learn to forgive, learn from the situation, and move on.

If we want to make things right, we need to stay away from wrath because wrath is not concerned with restoration but with revenge and dominance. So we need the type of forgiveness that restores the belief that we have power over what happens in our own lives. Naturally, things like holding grudges, only perpetuate a never-ending cycle of bad relationships which are diametrically opposed to having real community life.

Dante Alghieri, an Italian poet, writer, and philosopher, called wrath "a love of justice perverted to revenge and spite." It takes no intelligence or goodness of the soul to strike at those who hurt us. However, let us work more carefully on our souls and try to be better human beings. Know that one thing is quite sure; wrath also plays on our weaknesses.

Gluttony

Then, there is gluttony. It is greed, mass consumption, or just being hungry for power. All of these elements point to selfishness, which is the direct opposite of even a desire for community life. Gluttony is losing your sensitivity or temperance for distinguishing between what is enough and a respect for balance. As our grandparents used to say, "That's just being outright greedy, period." A person who has very little consideration for others.

It is also an excessive indulgence for short term, instant gratification. In addition, it is a sure sign of overpowering extreme self-love, which leaves little room for concern with others' needs. In addition, people like this just want to lord over everybody. Which reminds us of a principle the honorable Elijah Muhammad tried to inculcate or spread among his followers: "no big "I's or little you's." Moralists have long said that addiction to one's fleshly pleasures leads to other addictions.

Those who consume more than they need deny the excess to others. In addition, in a world like ours, where human beings die from lack of food, water, and medicine, the gluttony of a culture or an individual can mean death for those who hunger for our table scraps. So control your appetite and share more of what is beyond your needs. In addition, as our leader Imam W.D. Mohammed taught us, "Stop being such a wasteful people."

Thus, gluttony is also the excessive consumption that deprives another human being of a life-giving necessity. So taking more than your share of a certain resource or getting a third car when one will do; additionally, taking a third drink when one is best are good examples of gluttony.

Let us also remember that the skinny suffers from gluttony as easily and as often as the stout. For gluttony is primarily—excessiveness…so the opposite of gluttony is balance and consideration. It doesn't make a difference whether we are fat or skinny, wealthy or poor; gluttony can affect us all—if we let it in.

The excessive lifestyle of just American Christians— very few of whom lack basic provisions—is indirectly straining the rest of our planet. Just the same as Americans, period, we are an extremely wasteful nation. We throw away more food than any nation. Therefore, while building community, we have to stay away from wasteful tendencies.

Moreover, the question in light of our own glutinous tendencies is how much do you and I really need? What is a healthy basic lifestyle, and what is simply excessive? When you begin to demand more than you need, you are bordering on gluttony. If a community is to grow in a balanced format, it has to push the idea of needs first, wants last. This habit has to be reinforced regularly.

Gluttony is the sin that rides on the back of the other deadly sins. No matter what the sin is, greed or gluttony has its influence. This sin influences other sins. For example, gluttony sharpens the saw of sin and leads to all kinds of negative results. Pride longs for applause. However, gluttony counts no insignificant detail. It is enough to be slothful, but gluttony abandons virtue in excess.

Gluttony is salt when the greedy taste their spoils. One million dollars is not enough; it must be ten million. A person that is affected like this never has enough, he or she always wants more. For instance, lust wants another woman; gluttony wants them all. Wrath wants revenge; gluttony wants the infliction of it to be creatively painful. It is most demonic because gluttony amplifies the other sins, enhancing their self-destructive power.

Greed

Greed is another potential sin. Greed is inordinate love and devotion to wealth and accumulation. It is not enough to just have more, but a greedy person wants it all (i.e., resources, attention, and etc.). Greed is a form of worship because it dominates people's lives and demands. An obedience tantamount to slavery. Greedy individuals want you at their beck and call. They want their every request fulfilled.

Can people avoid this type of slavery in an unchecked capitalistic system? Yes, we can. But we will have to develop and maintain as much control over the life of our community as possible. If not, we will be caught up in the oldest game out there—unchecked capitalism. (i.e., get all you can, can all you get, and sit on the can). The real problem that greed imposes is not so much on the level of individual morality, but the sin of greed is a power over the structure of society as a whole.

It is a cultural adaptation. If it has not been checked enough on this level, greed becomes idolatry, a form of worship, because it turns people into slaves of their habit and addiction. They always want more. This turns into a lifestyle worship, the happy carefree feeling of limitless life and "lucre." The lyrics from the song "Summertime" by George Gershwin in the musical *Porgy and Bess* illustrate this well. For example, "It's summertime and the living is easy—fish are jumping and the cotton is high. Your daddy's rich and your mama's good-looking, so hush, little baby, don't you cry." This is true in some eyes because they think they have it all!

In order to counter this type of destructive energy, we need to get back to promoting the original meaning of the word *economy*, which is household management. The word *economy* can be traced back to Greek words, which mean "one who manages a household; manage, distribute by way of household management." Economy is later recorded as meaning "thrift" and "administration." However, we should also take heed of the current meaning: being careful with your resources. We must start a revolution of promoting and living a balanced life, not going to one extreme or the other. And we must develop an attitude that says: "let me get what I need more than what I want."

G-D's servant, Jesus Christ said, "That the affluent, those who have not shared what G-D has given them with the desperately impoverished, are a wretched lot." Their greed is a condition of their heart. A major sign of greed is that it adores goods that are temporary and resists those that are everlasting. Consequently, greed tends to influence people to go for the fast money and the easy things. They avoid the good things that take time to grow and develop. We need to check our attitude toward our fellow human beings. We need to become more charitable and loving toward one another.

What we tear down and rebuild says everything about our souls, our future, and the things we really value. We can tear down our current lifestyle and rebuild a new one filled with generosity. Alternatively, we can tear down the homes that have kept us more than comfortable and reinvent newer, bigger ones to replace them, with what we really do not need. Excess is not given for us to hoard. Excess is given that we may become extravagant gift givers—just like G-D instructed. In this way, the merciful and generous reflect their Creator. They become what they were always meant to be, servants of G-D.

On the other hand, the greedy show themselves devoid of such life. Lacking the only thing that matters—a purified soul. For as Jesus taught, "What good will it be for you to gain the whole world yet forfeit your soul." Jesus, G-D's servant, said that for everyone who has been given much, much will be demanded. And from the one who has been entrusted with much more, much more will be asked.

Sloth

Sloth is a life without ambition. Sloth is excessive attachment to the "old self"—making commitment to and finding joy in the "new self" difficult and distasteful. Sloth is also being indifferent toward neighbor, my soul, my world, and my G-D. Sloth moves us away from everything that ultimately matters, like being indifferent toward neighbors, the soul, the world, and the Creator. And it directs us toward simple distractions. Community building requires us to be, for the most part, moving in the same direction, sustaining our momentum, and upholding our values. Sloth is not mere laziness. It is indifference. Sloth is not restfulness; it is escapism of the deadly type.

Needless to say, developing a community requires that we keep our priorities in order as we move forward. Sloth leaves scant energy for our marriage or children or other duties. Another term for this is procrastination, when we waste valuable energies and time. Sloth is having a lazy attitude but gets excitement from petty matters. You know this when you are around irresponsible, carefree people. Sloth saps our energy and emotions through a favorite sports team, a new pair of shoes, or people because slothful individuals are not serious about important matters. I once heard someone say, "It is a monstrous thing to see one and the same heart at once so sensitive to minor things and so strangely insensitive to the greatest" (Blaise Paschal). *Allahu Akbar!*

The result is that we develop a lifestyle of investing valuable time in trivial matters and end up wasting important time in our lives and the life of our community. This attitude of ignoring our souls will keep us unconscious of the life G-D created for us, which is community life at its best. Finally, sloth will praise the holes we dig for ourselves. Even when we know they are unhealthy, sloth will tell us this is just the way life is. However, it is all an illusion, a mindset of not wanting to face reality. So always keep it real, and do not believe in the hyped-up lifestyle of the reckless and irresponsible people.

Vainglory

Vainglory is having a big ego. Vainglory is the opposite of the spirit you need for community building because excessive or ostentatious pride, especially in one's achievements, can get a people off balance and cause many problems. Vainglory is the opposite of humbleness, humility, and modesty. Believers must keep away from vainglory in building community life.

Vainglory, like pride, is an obsession with self and is the defining mark of a disintegrating soul. In addition, we cannot let selfishness exist when we are on a mission to establish community life. Vainglory is all about what selfish individuals think and want, not about what the community needs. In addition, thinking like this will not work when we are on a mission to accomplish something great and noble. Unlike other sins, pride usually appears when a person is at her or his best and allows that feeling of pride to go to the extreme. It is the same with vainglory. Although we need to know our strengths and other good qualities, it is just as important that we know our faults and weaknesses.

Pride is not viewing one's skills highly or possessing extra ordinary talents or displaying your talent for the benefit of others. Pride, instead, pushes or influences people to view themselves as the only one in the entire world who matters. Pride is not thinking too much of myself, pride is thinking of myself far too much. Pride loves the masks that hides our lonesome faces, and it disables a person from acknowledging their faults and flaws. Pride insists that we are just fine and tells us that no one will respect us if we expose the times and places where we have failed. Pride could be a very dangerous friend when everyone is trying to locate an organizational problem, and nobody is saying anything because it points to him or her! The problem is with one individual, and he/she is not admitting to it.

Pride also destroys our ability to connect with others because we are always thinking we are better than others are. What we say and do is more important than what others say or do. Pride reveals the natural love for self, magnified and perverted into disdain for others. This is a good example of extreme selfishness and can destroy any community building efforts. Pride prefers isolation to getting into heaven. An arrogant person lies and deceives and thinks nobody knows, but G-D knows!

It is a self-centered attitude that takes priority over contributions from others. In addition, it does not matter how important their contribution is. That is why we have to remember what our purpose is, which is to serve G-D and be of service to humankind. That's why getting rid of false pride is essential in order for us to get closer to our destiny as human beings, which is the establishment of community life. Moreover, pride or arrogance is Satan's flaw, which he revealed upon the creation of Adam (peace and blessings of G-D be upon him). And it earned him G-D's wrath.

Envy

Envy is the rejection of the good life that G-D has given me for an obsession with what G-D has given to someone else. This is jealousy, and jealousy is a major driving force behind envy. Also, envy makes people think that the life they have is worthless, so they do whatever they can to escape it. As we are pursuing community life, we cannot allow ourselves to be dragged down because we do not like that others have what we don't.

Even further, envy points to the good things that other people have while hiding the difficulties these people face. Envy also tells us that our lives are not valuable because we do not have more money, more toys, more acclaim, more privileges, or more so-called success than others. Consequently, envy encourages us to define our lives based on the number of material possessions we have and not on how well we treat ourselves, other people, and the blessings that G-D has bestowed upon us.

For example, the envy of the ancient Israelites led them to reject their identity. They wanted to worship a G-D king, like others around them. They would not accept their chosen position. When an individual is building his life, it is not productive to be looking over his shoulder to see if another person has more. The focus has to be on developing his individual and community life. So when the Israelites no longer knew who they were, the nation split and was conquered. In addition, they were forced off their land and exiled.

Another example is the story of Cain and Abel. Cain was envious of his brother Abel—and envy led to the murder of Abel and to Cain's exile. Envy's three favorite words are "why not me?" The answer is simple—their lives are not mine, and my life is not theirs. They are growing up in different ways and with different struggles. They may need to repair their own souls and develop their own talents in order to serve their community with what it needs. Therefore, people have to be concerned about themselves primarily in regard to the blessings that have been given to them, and do not preoccupy themselves wishing for the blessings of others. Nevertheless, the main concern has to be about our own community. Other people and individuals are not on our path, and we are not on theirs. They need a different kind of surgery, yet envy rejects such answers

These are the seven expressions plus one of the power of sin at work in our world. In addition, they are the seven plus one ways we hurt or assault those around us and around the world. Becoming a victim to any of these sins is destructive. If these seven deadly sins, plus one, gain a significant influence in our hearts and minds, the results are soul altering. They will destroy all that was once beautiful in us until we become a Frankenstein monster (a creation with multiple dark personalities) or something much worse. The sure way to counter the influence of the seven deadly sins is to inculcate in our lives The Seven Cardinal Virtues Plus One.

The virtues are as follows:

1. Faith: complete trust, showing a strong sense of duty or responsibility. Also being constant and loyal.
2. Hope: to be able to trust or rely on. A desire accompanied by expectation. A feeling that what is wanted may happen.
3. Love: an expression of one's affection. A feeling of goodwill and brotherhood toward other people. A devotion to and respect for G-D as the supreme being.
4. Practical wisdom: taking the premise to its logical conclusion. It is the power of judging rightly and following the soundest course of action. Not doing this haphazardly or emotionally but coming up with a strong, lasting life plan.
5. Justice: to be fair to "oneself and others even if it may be against yourselves, your parents, or close relatives, be they rich or poor;" to come correct and true; to have sound reasoning and righteous intentions.
6. Courage: to have an attitude and a spirit (mind, heart, and soul) to deal with anything that is dangerous or painful, without withdrawing. Additionally, courage is having the tenacity to stay focused on community-building efforts for the long haul despite facing obstacles from generation to generation. Courage is doing what is right.

7. Temperance: taking a sober, moderate approach in speech and action. Having a measured degree of self-restraint in the conducting of affairs. Knowing how to remain civil at all times during this long and trying process of establishing community life.
8. Humility: no big I's or little you's but gratitude for G-D's favors. I am no greater or lesser than anyone else. I possess the dignity of *khalifah*.

When you go against these cardinal virtues, you are opening the door to some or all of the seven deadly sins plus one because developing the virtues is G-D allowing you to protect yourself from the effects or influence of the deadly sins. We must always be diligent in developing and protecting our soul. Therefore, we should not accept anything that is unethical as we build community life. Because when we lower our standards, we open the door to evil and other negative influences.

Imam W.D. Mohammed points out how we, African American people, less than 150 years out of slavery, have lost our sense of social life and being a social community.

> We have lost our southern moral sense and our social sense. We had a social sense of how we should live with each other. And we had a moral sense of how we should live with each other. And we had more unity and more respect to support our progressing as a people then, than we have right now, today at this late hour. This is

plain. It is very clear to you how we have degraded ourselves as a people after being freed from slavery in the South.

Imam Mohammed continues his analysis of our rejection of the African American moral and social sense:

The Shaitan's plan, the plan that worked— that white southern man didn't conceive that plan... That plan was conceived by Shaitan himself; the devil conceived how to create racism—turn blacks against whites and whites against blacks and how to enslave the blacks and anticipated them one day being freed and being in a condition spiritually, in a condition mentally to be manipulated by the Shaitan himself and eventually become the influence to bring all people down. And whose spirit is the Shaitan using to reach the whole cultural world and bring mankind down? He is using the Negro spirit; excuse me but I want it plain. He's using the black man's spirit. He's using the Afro American spirit. He's using the African American spirit... It's terrible, but it's true and it's real. And Allah has shown it to Elijah Muhammad's son. For what? So, we can survive and prosper in spite of the works of Satan, so powerful and so prevalent in the greatest country

in the world, the United States of America.
Here is the greatest progress for human freedom and democracy, and here is the greatest progress for Satan's freedom. (Ramadan
Session, October 6, 2007, part 2).

According to Imam Mohammed, African Americans
have submitted to the immoral life that America provides
and are spreading that immoral behavior through entertainment, which is being embraced around the world. Accepting
"Satan's freedom" as an unprincipled, immoral people will
destroy all likelihood of building a model community and
achieving the great destiny that G-D has for us.

The following are some of the cardinal virtues and
their counterparts: practical wisdom perfects the intellect; justice perfects the will. In addition, courage perfects
the part of the soul that deals with emotions like fear and
hope. Temperance perfects the part of the soul that deals
with feelings of desire and pleasure. So as I said, developing
these virtues puts us in a much better position to realize
a successful community life. Furthermore, the theological
virtue of faith elevates the intellect to a divine level.

While the virtue of hope and charity directs the will
beyond human good to G-D. When people are G-D conscious, we can expect cooperation and a good-hearted effort
toward community life. So developing these virtues puts us
in much better shape to realize successful community life.
Because the intellect and will comprise our rational nature,
all aspects of the human being's rationality are perfected by
these virtues.

The moral of the story is to be conscious of both sin and virtue in our lives as we pursue our responsibility—COMMUNITY LIFE.

IWDM's language
Code or decode—I think not

We don't need for any individual or group to decode Imam W. Deen Mohammed's *tafsir* for us. The *Imam's* explanation of concepts is crystal clear, and we thank him for it. For now, all we have to do is put it into action and stop thinking so much while our adversaries are busy attacking us and planning our demise. We are, some of us, busy reading too much into things (or not enough); seek the balance!

Imam Mohammed finished thirty-three or more years of successful surgery on us. The patient has been healed for the most part. Now, all that is left to do is to live this refined life in all its aspects: spiritually, culturally, economically, and educationally as brothers and sisters from the same womb. This is the way the whole society benefits. It's community building time.

Let's not neglect our roots. If we want to take time structuring national *shuras* (Consultative Body) and such, we should try to involve all of us or the whole community. The *Imam* stressed that the whole community becomes vulnerable in the schemes of *shaitan* when we try to police one another too much. A hint to the wise is sufficient. So let local leadership handle local issues and form local *shuras*. This way it frees people and communities up to exercise "autonomy" when it comes to local issues and concerns. Our leader was very clear on this. Study his articles regarding the *shuras*.

When a national concern arises, I think a representative from each regional *shuras* should weigh in on that concern. We would be free, however, to follow our own conscience if there is more than one righteous approach to the issue. The *shuras* could do this through courteous communication, which we should do anyway.

Imam W. Deen Mohammed advised us to go back to our local communities, work, get strong, and build up our community life. We need to get away from the age-old problem of "too much talk and not enough work and appreciation for what has preceded us. Let's think! The Qur'an says, "Thinking benefits man." Again, we don't need for any individual or group to decode Imam W. Deen Mohammed's *tafsir* for us.

Our common interfaith challenge

The focus is to follow G-D's way (i.e., Judaism, Christianity, and Al-Islam), not our personal way. We, all G-D-fearing people, have the same objective—to please the one and only Creator who fashioned the heavens and the earth and all in between.

This creation was in progress just as G-D was bringing his man to his noble position as a leader or vicegerent in the world through the great prophets of G-D, such as Adam, Abraham, Jesus, Moses, and Mohammed, and etc. So let us not let Satan influence or direct our actions any

further. Unity is the only objective of the G-D-fearing people, no matter what faith we profess. When we meet, we
need to stay close to the basic principles that unite us, and
stay away from personal cultural edicts that present a negative influence on others.

If we profess to be G-D-fearing people, we must learn
how to show more respect for revelation and the contin-
uum of G-D's guidance on all G-D-fearing people. We
must stop letting Satan divide us. There is an old saying
that says, "the devil is in the details." Well, that includes the
details of religious knowledge also.

We need to humble ourselves a little more and try
harder to be more understanding and sincerely curious
toward other good peoples of the world. What, do you
think G-D gave one community the only patent on being
human? I don't think so! Who knows, if we take a closer
look, we may learn something valuable. For Allah says in
the Holy Qur'an,

> O humanity! Indeed! We created you
> from a male and a female and made you
> into peoples and tribes so that you may
> get to know one another. Surely, the most
> noble of you in the sight of G-D is the
> most righteous among you. G-D is truly
> All-Knowing, All-Aware. (49:13)

Do you know that G-D made our very fingertips different from the next person's? If we take the narrow approach
and think that we have all the answers, we open the door

for Satan and his dupes to come in our midst. Moreover, everybody is not going to be the same, so we might as well explore this unity challenge.

We must be true to ourselves, and true religion is for the faithful and intelligent mind. It's not for a mind that gives itself to emotions. Everything that G-D has established for us is for a good reason, and we just have to learn to follow the knowledge to its logical conclusion.

Let us all begin to look to the higher truths in matters of religion, not just what we literally read with no understanding. If we don't know something, we must ask somebody who does know, or at least ask someone who can point us in the right direction.

Let's at least come together in dialogue and work to make an effort to print and speak about the common principles that G-D gave us all and apply them. Some of our most basic common principles are:

- We (the sincere ones) all believe in one supreme being (Creator) that controls the heavens and earth.
- We all want the best future for our children.
- We all want the best for the human being and the planet.

If we practice these common principles, the day will come sooner than later (G-D willing) where we will realize real peace and progress in the world, more appreciation and love for one another, less war talk and more peace talk, and etc. We can't afford anything less!

The growth and development of our history

The community of Imam W. Deen Mohammed has evolved in three major stages:

STAGE 1: 1930–1975 represents "The Nation of Islam." During this stage, believers were introduced to the basic concepts and language of Al-Islam in a community structure that was designed to "build a nation" while improving the moral, social, and economic conditions of the believers.

The leadership was from the top down. This was a time when believers were dependent on the headquarters of the Honorable Elijah Muhammad (RAA) and his leadership team to sanction their local activities.

STAGE 2: The second stage of development (1975–2008) represents the leadership of Imam W. Deen Mohammed (RAA). This period exemplifies development into the fullness and purity of Islamic life. Imam Mohammed transitioned members of the Nation of Islam into a new Islamic consciousness based upon the guidance of the Holy Qur'an, life example of Mohammed the prophet (PBUH), principles of natural thinking (Deen-ul-fitra), and the unique blessing from Allah that allowed him to wake up that natural inclination within believers to serve their Creator and put them on the destiny toward community life.

Inherent in this transformation was the freedom to develop natural Islamic community life from the bottom up. We didn't have a lord and dictators over us telling us every move to make (i.e., when to pray, eat, go to bed, study, etc.). We learned to do it on our own. As a result, Imam Mohammed freed local communities and believers to develop independent and autonomous governing structures and hold ourselves accountable for the leadership and governance of community life.

The *Imam* also introduced the concept and models of Islamic Democracy and *Amruhum Shuraa Baynahum* (Governance by mutual consultation) to guide our ability to make collective decisions.

He also gave us the vision for community life as a direction for our community and explained the four things that we would have to develop in order to attain Islamic community life: the four birds metaphor of education, economics, culture, and government

STAGE 3: The third and present stage (2008–present) represents the natural growth and maturity of Islamic community life. In this natural progression, autonomous and independent leaders and local communities have been blessed with an eighty-eight year (plus) legacy of leadership, guidance, and evolution of our community. As we continue to progress, the Qur'an, the example of Prophet Muhammad (PBUH), and the thinking of our Imam should guide this development. So as men and women of consciousness, we should feel an obligation to Allah, to our history, and to the legacy of our Imam and our community.

Therefore, we will not stand by and let corrupt usurpers and/or pretenders insert themselves into our community and disrupt this natural progression. Our community has been blessed. Let's recognize this blessing before it's too late. Remember, the Honorable Elijah Muhammad (RAA) says, "No big I's and little you's." We know what that leads to.

"RECONSTRUCTION"…minus immorality.
Let's make it live again, in our communities,
in all its aspects with sustainability.

CHAPTER 5

Growth and Development

Consult each other on matters regarding community life. This is a commentary on the responsibilities of the consultative body of the Muslim Community (our community). The *shura* or consultative body of this community (those in the association of Imam W. Deen Mohammed) has been in existence for a few years. During these past few years, the body of his community has only heard from this *shura* when noticeable events are going on, like the annual convention or an international issue of critical concern to the world occurs, such as terrorism or a natural disaster. We need to hear from this body more often. Therefore, in order for us to be knowledgeable of the workings and operations of the shura, we need periodic or quarterly reports. I think that the *shura* will agree with this premise that the community can only make educated assessments of the progress that is attempted and accomplished by the *shura*, when we are properly informed.

We need to hear from this body more often. They should be issuing opinions that reflect our leadership and community's position on everything of importance to the Muslim community. We should even know about their regular meetings and when they are to be held.

The *shura* should be made up of individuals who have good character, who are knowledgeable in the faith, and who have a decent track record of working on behalf of our community. Moreover, the shura should also have persons on the board that work in the outer community. So that when issues come up that can potentially affect the Islamic community in any way, we will have someone who has established him or herself in other fields of endeavor to give an educated view on the matter from an Islamic perspective, as well as provide professional expertise in the decision-making of the board.

Additionally, the community needs periodic reports on exactly what the *shura* is involved in so that our community can always be well-informed. The *shura* can do this by extending its responsibility and sponsoring regular educational seminars in the outer community. This will help to educate us on the *tafsir* of our late leader Imam W. Deen Mohammed regarding issues that he has weighed in on, such as economics, social life, family, education, etc.

The *shura* should renew its vigor and sense of purpose by setting up and attending biannual recreational retreats. This will serve to help them recreate themselves and motivate them to redouble their efforts at building model communities that reflect the wisdom of Imam W. Deen Mohammed (RAA), the example of Prophet Muhammad (SAW), and the plan of Allah (SWT).

It is well-known that every good organization has its checks and balances. So I would recommend that the *shura* have time limits on serving as a member of the shura board, like the governmental structures of the United States of America. More importantly, if the body becomes ineffective, limited terms of service would curtail their impact upon the community.

Furthermore, we encourage the *shura* to try to always work together as a solid unit and avoid the tendency that is in all of us at times—to be individually or selfishly oriented. I remember our late leader Imam W. Deen Mohammed (RAA) saying once in the nation's capital that when talking about picking someone for a position of responsibility, if he had to choose between a person that was knowledgeable, had skills, and was sincere and another who had knowledge, skills, and was versed in Al-Islam but was of questionable character, he said that he would pick the first person.

Another example of this scenario would be choosing between someone versed in the Qur'an, makes all of his prayers but is arrogant toward others and spends all of his time in the *masjid* and another who is dedicated to learning the Qur'an, is not arrogant, and spends most of his time out in the community with the people and treats others in the way that he would like to be treated, which one would you choose?

Imam W. Deen Mohammed (RAA) said in Detroit in July 1995 that we should not close our eyes when trying to make an assessment of a matter. He advised us that we should seek guidance from the Qur'an and from the higher authority of Allah and his prophets (peace be upon them). He said: "Our prophet was a very rational and very considerate person. He was not bull-headed. He was not stubborn in his opinions. He was the prophet of G-D, and G-D gave him revelation and guidance. And if he was asked something and he thought that someone had experience or knowledge about it, he would consult him." That is the kind of person Prophet Muhammad (PBUH) was. Likewise, let us strive to be that way. Let us not be so stiff, so dogmatic, so opinionated, and inhumane. But let us try to be like the prophet, our model—a human person, a human man, a human leader.

Finally, this commentary is to say that whether we are a member of a committee or the *shura* or any decision-making body in this community, we should adopt this type of spirit—a consultative spirit. And I hope this advice is useful.

"Brotherhood—Respect It and Follow Leadership"

CHAPTER 6

Social Responsibility/Young People

Excerpts taken from a lecture entitled "Support Religion for Social Dignity and Community Empowerment" given on March 14, 2008, by Imam W. Deen Mohammed

The Muslim agenda is based upon what Allah (SWT) has revealed to us as our responsibility in the Qur'an and in the life of His Servant Messenger Muhammad, the prayers and the peace be upon him.

We think the topic, the subject that we are addressing here, is a subject that really needs to be represented to the general society of America. Particularly to the African American people in the society of this country, whether they believe like we do or not in religion. Because we, more than any other people, have unusual kinds of problems or peculiar difficulties coming to grips with or accepting social responsibility.

Social responsibility

The word *social* refers directly to human relationships in society. The first social obligation is to one's closest members, our families. But the social obligation extends outside of your family community into the general community.

Three circles

I would say for people who try to establish their lives in accordance, with the ideas that they have in their religion, should know that there are three circles that they have to be aware of, as circles for their lives and their livelihood. The first being the family, the second would be their religious community, and the third would be the general community. That is the situation for us. We have to be concerned for our families first, then for the Muslim community, and lastly, for the general community, the city, beginning with the neighborhoods where we live because it is non-Muslim. However, I don't think we have any Muslim neighborhoods yet. But we hope to have them soon. So you have to begin with your neighborhood and most likely, even with your neighbor next door.

What Islam wants for us

I think this topic is one that needs more discussion openly, publicly that is, not just in institutions. We know these institutions are working on social problems, and they also create problems; not that we are not doing wrong ourselves. We make mistakes too because we are not in the light. We have those three circles, and two of those circles belong to us as Muslims—our families and our Muslim community. We should be striving to do everything possible to establish social responsibility for ourselves as individuals, for our families, and for our Muslim communities. That's what Islam wants for us.

Now, in perceiving the society, the interest of the society, it's very simple. The interest is to perceive ourselves first as social creatures. When Allah tells us over and over again in Qur'an that He made us as plants. Plants also have male and female, that causes them to generate and grow together. That's how they grow best. When you put certain types of grass to itself and keep other grasses out, that grass thrives best. So even the plant life thrives best when it congregates or when it hangs out together.

If it gets mixed up with each other, you find weeds on everything, killing and strangling its life. But when they grow together, they grow nicely. If you put foreign plants as close as you put plants of the same life form, you will not be able to get the abundance of growth that you'll get if you let those plants grow just to themselves.

So that's what Allah is telling us. That life should be with its kind, and certainly, the corrupt should not be mixed all in with non-corrupt. If we are clean and decent, we don't want to have non-decent people mixed all among us.

In fact, if I could, I would have them sitting in a certain spot somewhere else. But we can't. G-D has given us no authority. Instruction from the Prophet (PBUH) is that we don't have authority to look into their hearts and minds and determine the value of them. Allah knows their value; we can't judge that.

So now, what do we have to see first? That Al-Islam is a religion that focuses the light on man and shows him firstly, principally, as a social creature and that G-D intended for him to be a social creature. He is not to be satisfied being an island or on an island all to himself. He must mate and become a bigger social unit, made up of family and tribes until he embraces the whole community of man on this earth and himself as a member in one family with all people.

Qur'an gives social inspiration

Since man is a social creature, then the spirit of the Qur'an is social inspiration. It feeds our social aspirations. So this word *social* is bigger that we think it is. By social, we don't mean just associating with each other physically but by our dependency to each other as members of a world community. But we want to keep the focus on the Muslim community right now. As members of the Muslim community, our dependency on each other and our love for each other brings us together.

Pretty soon, we find that the teacher in the schools has to be tied full-time in doing that. But there is also a need to have business growing in the community. So that means that we must have business people in the community addressing that need.

The social context in terms of people keeps expanding with growth, and as it grows, there is more demand for more things to take care of the needs of its growing people. He can have the regulation of the home in the parent. He can have the regulation of the family in the parent. He can have the regulations of the morals in the parent. The laws that discipline the family can also be in the parent. All of those things can be done by the parent.

That's a small unit, and the parent can manage that. But when it extends and involves hundreds of families, he can't manage that. If there is nobody but him and his family, he can go out and take his sons and children with him, plow the field, and regulate his own food. He doesn't need anyone to regulate that economy for him. He can handle that himself. But when they multiply in a social unit, it's the social unit that is getting bigger. As the social unit gets bigger, it brings on demands for industry, more sophisticated government, and more complex governmental ideas that sustain itself. There is not one other single influence responsible for the growth and development of society other than the social principle or social influence.

Now, let us look at the sun as a symbol. The sun is the principal influence behind all the changes in the weather and the colors and the growth of everything. Likewise, the social interest principle is the influence behind all the other growth and possibilities.

Social dignity

We are also talking about religion and how religion offers support to the community for community empowerment and what it offers also for economic dignity. But I would say the motivation for economic dignity in the plan of G-D is the social dignity and the social honor.

G-D says that He has created everything in honorable pairs, also translated to mean noble pairs. Nobility means a lot to men and women of intellect. G-D says that He made honorable every son and child of Adam, both male and female. And when the two come together, they represent the social interest in this language. So there is proof in revelation that the social interest is our nature. This takes away the macho insanity. He says that He made us one from another—from one person, from one soul. *Nafs* means soul, but it also means person.

The beginning of the great construction of this democracy that has outlived every other form of democracy and government until now is really a kind of beacon light for the rest of the world. Right now, it is serving as that. We have other nations coming under pressure to bring their democracy, or accept democracy, so that their democracies won't shame man on earth.

Not that we are satisfied with this democracy, it doesn't mean that at all, but I am just pointing to that. What I am pointing at is the movement to construct this great idea of democracy started with the social principle.

Politics comes from man's social aspirations

Man is identified as a social entity by nature. Inherently, he is a social creature, not a political creature, and it is his social interest that solicits or requisitions the political establishment and every other establishment. So if we neglect the social life, the social dignity of our community, we are aborting all of those other great possibilities, aren't we? Because the first womb is the social interest, it's going to give birth to all the others. So if we don't attend the first womb, the first mother, we are aborting our other great possibilities.

So I think I'm giving you keys for making your community a productive and progressive community. Now, maybe I'm dreaming and I'm not in the world of reality myself, but I don't think so. You all have to wake me up if I'm dreaming, but I think I'm awake. What I told you is simple. I told the brothers when I was coming down, I said, "There shouldn't be many questions when I finish because my plan is to make it so clear no one will have a question."

That's what I tried to do. And I have brought you to the point where I wanted to bring you, and I can say what I want to say now away from the subject but yet in connection with the subject with no difficulty whatsoever.

We must be different. We can't go on being just like we used to be in the past. We must be different from the majority of the African American people. We must not follow in their pattern of behavior. We must not follow in their moral behavior. We must not follow them in their business behavior.

We must take on a new business behavior, and we must demand that we have business people in our community, that can supply us our needs, our grocery needs, our clothing needs, or all of our needs. We should put pressure on them. Say, "Brother, you are qualified. Brother, you have so much education. Brother, why don't you go back to school and complete that education, or why don't you take the education you have now and go get some specific knowledge in this particular area? We think you can be a good grocery store operator. We think you can be a good banker or good financier."

Let us put pressure on our people that have promise that tells us by way of qualification, that they can do more for us than they are doing. Let's tell them that you have an obligation to produce not just for yourself, brother. Your interest is community as well.

Allah (SWT) created you for community interest. The community is a social entity by the nature. That G-D gave it and created you, brother, to contribute something to your community and to provide for your community.

Business: start where you can and be methodical and patient

We are supposed to be providers, and to provide, you must have something. So that means you have to own something. You have to be responsible for something. You have to make it produce and come up with the supplies or the provisions that the community must depend on. We can start with simple things, with easy things. Start where we can start. I don't believe in going after the impossibility and stepping over the possibility. That's stupid. But a lot of our degreed people will do just that. You come up with a simple vision, and they will make it so damn complicated. Excuse the language…that it will make you go home, and you will have locked bowels for two weeks.

Say, what happened to the beautiful idea we had? We don't want that. This world will give our people practical knowledge. But they give them so much imagination, theory, and dreams in terms of where they can go individually, so much so that they forget to put the interest first on the tools that they have to use to get where they want to go. And they put all the attention on the mirror that looks like the picture of how I'm going to look when I get there. And they can never get there because they can't stop looking at themselves, thinking about what they are going to be when they get there.

African Americans must support one another

Support African American business, and start first, if you are Muslim, with your own Muslim brother. Support your African American Muslim brother's business. And if there are any non-African American Muslim brothers in your congregation, make no distinction between them. They are just like the black one. They are in your congregation. Once a brother is in our neighborhood, or in our congregation, no color matters at all. He's with us. The brotherhood of Islam is more powerful than the brotherhood of blood or race. So you make no distinction if he is in your community. But if he is outside of your community, why help the *Jingolese?* There is no such thing as *Jingolese.* Don't look it up. It's not even in the dictionary. Why help the *Jingolese* Muslim community and you belong to the African American Muslim community?

Is your community so strong and so solid that it can now give aid to the *Jingolese* community? Or do you need aid? You keep your efforts here. Support yourself and build yourself up strong so that your hand will not be like that (palm up). Your hand will be like that (palm down) one day. And that's the honor, so says our prophet (prayers and peace be on him). That's the honor, being able to give to somebody else and then help bring them up.

So this is what I want to see. I want to see the Muslim community continue to have an interest in the outer community, grow in government, grow in politics of this area, grow in business, and support your good business people.

Brain trust

Business people should form an association. You already have it here and in some other places, but I'm telling you again because maybe some here are not with you. Business people should form an association that will not jeopardize the members of the club, or the members of the association, but bring the members together, so they can benefit from each other's resources.

And what I'm talking about most of all are the mental resources, intellectual resources, and brain resources. Come together so you can benefit from each other's experiences because the knowledge that is missing in you and perhaps even those working immediately with you, may be with another brother that belongs to your congregation.

When you all come together and share freely with each other, without charging each other anything but benefitting mutually, you are having social interaction on a higher level than just entertainment, eating, or dining. This is the most productive level of social interaction, and you are benefitting, multiplying, and growing.

There is much I would like to say to you. I could talk until this time tomorrow, and I won't finish. G-D knows it. But I have to go, and you have to go. Thank you very much. May Allah forgive us our shortcomings and our sins and grant us mercy and guidance always. Amen.

Social responsibility: the moral mis-authority. No more of this, "a perspective"

The leadership and good people have allowed a pattern of behavior and a negatively influenced moral and ethical climate to dominate the social and psychological landscape of our society. This climate of disregard and disrespect for good morals and respectful behavior has influenced and damaged almost an entire generation. Most of our young people find it hard to determine between what is clearly wrong from what is clearly right.

This type of assault on the good rational senses (influences, morals, and values) of the human being are unacceptable. So we must fight this assault with our very souls, consciences, and resources.

We have to reestablish our sober love for one another and concern for our existence as intelligent human beings. In other words, we are going to have to promote and develop a mindset that says, whatever that is good that I love for myself, I must love the same things for my brothers and sisters.

Social responsibility: youth, and unifying our efforts

It is time that serious people organize for work, no matter how they define themselves. Speaking to our young people, some of you should form or belong to our youth organizations. Others, say around twenty-five to forty, should join the general body and contribute to and follow the initiatives and direction that Imam W. Deen Mohammed left for our community.

The leaders or *Imams* should encourage and support the efforts of the youth, but do not attempt to control them from behind the scenes. Imam Mohammed has advised that, "In our local community, the youthful adults, age twenty-five to forty, are not to advertise themselves as young adults in our community. They should identify members who are having the same interests that they have and are aggressive and invite them to join them and their efforts." An official local group can be very effective without always making a lot of noise.

Imam Mohammed also advised in his interview that these "youthful organizations," ages twelve to twenty, should seek the wise advice of some of the seasoned adults amongst our seniors when they have questions or concerns as they proceed in their activities.

Our leader, Imam W. Deen Mohammed, once said that the members of these groups should chose persons to lead them, that reflect the leader's initiatives and positions of this community.

I think the young adults need to hear the same or similar message from their local leaders—*Imams* from places like Florida, Atlanta, Los Angeles, Philadelphia, and etc. It is very important to show this community that they, the local *Imams*, support the *Imam's* position because it is a living and growing message. They could do things like write commentaries or speak out about the need for change as it relates to our young people.

Progress and peace are evolving phenomena. If we want them, they cost. Don't get it twisted; we are living in the last days and times. There will be nothing new, just the recycled. The same human DNA that the earth was born with is the same DNA now. Nothing new, just a different package. It is an honor and privilege to be a part of this organized human struggle we're in. This is a struggle for our very hearts and souls, as well as the minds of the human being as we know it.

Imam W. Deen Mohammed (RAA) in an African American Genesis says:

> The Holy Qur'an also addresses community responsibilities. God tells us, 'Hold firmly to the cable that God extends out to you (for your salvation, for your unity), and do not be divided among yourselves.' We have a community obligation to hold onto the Holy Qur'an, the Word of God. We have an obligation to hold on to Prophet Muhammad (PBUH), the last and universal liberator from God. We are obligated to hold on to his sunnah (practices). As stated in the above verse, we have an obligation to hold on to each other.

After all, God has extended His Help that we may be united. Muslims are to be united against the forces and schemes of Satan, which are divisive. Satan can break the unity of everybody except those who are united under God. (15)

So young people, never enter a situation in the middle of its struggle and think you know what's best without a complete understanding. You still need leadership to assist you. Therefore, come into community life with all the vigor, all the education, and all the sophistication you have. But come in a humble and patient manner. Come with a historical sense of respect for those who strove and struggled before you, but do not come to the situation with an air of arrogance or a disposition like you know it all when you haven't been tried and tested yet.

Young or youthful adults, you have a leader that was blessed with an insight that you don't have. That's why we call him leader—the one who sees out ahead of the body. You have to study and trust the leader's instincts to protect our community life. You need to follow and contribute all that you can and be patient. If something or someone tries to impede your righteous progress or your strategy, you are intelligent youthful adults, so go around it. Don't let talk or too much planning in meetings stop you from contributing in a real sense.

I heard Imam Mohammed say that the way things look, we are a couple of generations away from really establishing ourselves as a people. Therefore, I implore you to live in the present but plan for the future. Live locally but think globally. Between here and there, there is work to be done. Let's get busy!

From young to youthful to adults, it's past the time that we put away childish attitudes, dispositions, and ways of doing things. It's time to show our seriousness and maturity and get behind this solid leadership that Imam W. Deen Mohammed left with us and leave the naysayers and the nay doers alone. Your acceptance of responsibility will acknowledge appreciation for all the human struggles that brought us to this point and that went before you. For this reason, study your history and follow the best thereof in productivity. Peace!

Human lives matter

Human lives matter, which include black lives! We as African American men know the horrors and disrespect of police brutality and mistreatment. We are all too familiar with us being targeted because of our race and this exaggerated negative image of us being overly sexual and aggressive, and what this picture of us must do to the minds of the misinformed or ignorant public servants called policemen. With projected images like this being generated by the media and those of ill-intention, one can only conclude that this is done on purpose to make the public think and perceive that these guys pose a threat to the status quo. This image is grossly exaggerated, for we pose no bigger threat than the average male in America. But for some type of economic or cultural reason, maybe both, it is made to seem that way.

Perhaps, we need to study the effects of slavery and the psychology of oppression to try to understand the unfair hand that the black man has been dealt in this society. This approach will help shine some light on this problem of ignorance and fear that we find ourselves struggling with in our society today. Our people, especially our menfolk, have suffered more than any other segment of this population, and we ask and demand that our men be recognized as a central and respectable part of this American experiment. We've earned it, and we ask that you consciously increase the portrayal of black men in movies as strong, serious, moral characters that love their families and communities. Men that represent an integral part of this human race.

As a result, the issue at hand is that law enforcement officials are too aggressive when it comes to handling situations that involve black men. The facts and studies have verified this. Now, we just have to get busy correcting this false image and putting training programs in place to address this issue. Law enforcement and security organizations are going to have to go through some serious cultural and sensitivity education. Not just one seminar or class but I suggest an ongoing program in the pursuit of respecting human excellence because America is made up of different ethnicities and cultural groups that enrich our communities and this country.

Law enforcement will really have to seriously revisit and learn and study their age-old purpose to "protect and serve." Without a doubt, this job can be trying and dangerous at times, but it can also be rewarding to those who sincerely like to serve the public. However, if an officer is not genuine, he should choose another profession and do something that fits his true personality.

Now, for those of us who are behind the Black Lives Matter (BLM) Movement, they are absolutely correct. Black lives do matter, and our lives must matter to us more than anyone else. So when we think about this movement of Black Lives Matter, let us use this opportunity to address, the best we can, some of the internal systemic problems that we face as a people and that we need to address. We have to be bold and courageous enough to look at our own situation from all angles; therefore, what can we do as a by-product of this movement to show the world and ourselves that our lives matter more to us than anybody else and that we are willing to take the necessary steps to improve our lives? Looking at this concept wholistically, but not taking our eyes off of the current particular issues (BLM), following are some important things that we need to keep our minds on and resolve:

1. We need to identify and focus on the value system that brought us through slavery and part of this century—a commitment to get established and have and develop our own life in this country.
2. Our lack of business life in our communities.
3. The fact that we need to demonstrate more respect for one another.
4. The need for us to stop being reactionary and work with serious-minded people to develop a community plan; a plan that we will commit to and follow until we realize it.

5. Let's stop supporting businesses, entertainers, people, and products that don't, in some way, give back to the community.

6. We really need to focus on getting our health back. For example, we eat unhealthy foods; a lot of us are overweight, and we try to justify it. People, we can do better!

7. Let's set better standards and examples for our youth. We must revisit our good moral and ethical history, for crime has almost sucked the life out of our community. Thus, we must bring vibrancy back to our community.

8. Let's stop letting some of our people and others take advantage of us and exploit our community for their individual gains.

9. We must commit ourselves, if necessary, to two generations of building community life for the benefit of our children and the glory of G-D.

Let us take advantage of this introspection and actualization to really become productive and respected citizens of the United States of America.

From another angle, why is it that law enforcement officers use excessive force when encountering black males, women, and children? Yes, we are all aware of white supremacy and racism as factors for their behavior, but why has the justice system itself been reluctant to hold these individuals accountable?

Historically, the role of the police has been to keep marginalized groups under control—e.g., blacks, the poor, immigrants, and etc. Their job is to maintain the status quo, so it is not unusual to police unions and possibly the police administration when officers abuse people from those groups. And being marginalized means that they are outside the halls of power, yet they have not learned that their protection is in the power of the group or community that has learned to survive and thrive despite the forces/guardians of the status quo being arrayed against them.

A recent example of how politics and the justice system protect police is the killing and trial of George Floyd. The citizens of Minneapolis, Minnesota, witnessed the killing of George Floyd, an unarmed black man, when Officer Derek Chauvin, the training officer, knelt on Floyd's neck and back for nine minutes and twenty-nine seconds during an arrest where Floyd allegedly passed a counterfeit $20 bill. Due to local and international protests, an African American Attorney General, and many months later, Chauvin was found guilty of second-degree murder, third-degree murder, and second-degree manslaughter.

Yet this verdict was unexpected despite the video of the incident and police testimony against Derek Chauvin. And that shows how powerful police departments have become. The Minneapolis police union paid one million dollars for a twelve-lawyer team to defend Derek Chauvin, although he used excessive force which was outlawed by the police department itself. To complicate matters even further, the president of the Fraternal Order of Police gets his salary from local tax dollars.

In many extrajudicial killings, local district attorneys, who only prosecute criminal cases, do not even charge officers when police body cameras or local citizens record their excessive force, so that is why it is difficult to hold police and the justice system accountable because the policing structure is designed to control and contain marginalized groups like black men, not to "protect and serve" them. Ironically, days before the verdict of Derek Chauvin, a young black man was killed by another training officer in the state of Minnesota during a traffic stop. Until black people, as a community, have the means (i.e., businesses, culture, education, and government) to control their survival, they will be vulnerable and used in a manner for others to profit from. Then, and only then will black lives matter to us and to others.

When Prophet Muhammad (PBUH) and the believers began to build community life, G-D brought them many victories against those who attacked them. And when they became an established community in the land, instead of seeking vengeance, he asked that his former enemies accept the peace. He said, "Let the bloodletting stop. Spill no blood. And if you accept the peace, you have the same protection here that other citizens have. Have no fear for your property or for your lives."

Prophet Muhammad (PBUH) knew that he had to exercise kindness and justice toward all in order to maintain the peace. Likewise, may our system of justice understand that simple maxim so that black lives and other marginalized groups will "have no fear for their property or for their lives."

"Unity/Cooperation—If we are to be successful."

CHAPTER 7

Human Lives Matter

Advice to our youngsters
Be your own man (mind)—develop your character

Martin Luther King, Jr., encouraged character development. And Imam W. Deen Mohammed inspired us to think deeply and to control our emotionalism. Today, our preachers need to get back to addressing moral and ethical issues. However, what we, as a people, need to do is stop asking others to do for us that which we can do for ourselves and correct our own behavior.

The Advice

1. Always be honest and truthful.
2. Put your best effort forward—always do your best.
3. Show more concern for others.
4. Don't follow the trends; be your own man/woman.
5. Watch the company you keep.

6. Surround yourself with positive people who are trying to make life better for their families and communities.
7. Study your history as a people among other people and the lessons to be learned from the interaction.
8. Be a man, utilizing your mind, maintaining women, and taking on the responsibilities of community life.
9. Serve and protect your family and community.

Father-son relationship

Our sons require our love and support. Let's make our boys strong, the father-son relationship solutions. We want to share some suggestions for improving the father-son relationship:

1. Make some reserved time—at least once a week—where you and your son(s) can meet and talk. Where he can ask of you about life and anything that might be concerning him. You should encourage your son to express himself in his appropriate manner
2. Fathers should show more interest in the activities and projects that their sons are involved in. For example, if they are on the science team or the business club, then get involved in their projects. If they are in the band or participating in a sporting activity, then go to some of their practice sessions, games, and recitals.

3. It's our responsibility, as fathers, to get involved in the parent-teacher association at their schools. You will be surprised how much influence you can have by becoming a part of such organizations. This will help African American fathers achieve their goal of having a positive and lasting impact in their community through their children.

4. It's also very important that our sons see us having constructive and enjoyable interactions with their peers' parents and caregivers. In this way, they learn from us what is proper behavior and what is not. This approach has a dual effect: it makes us conscious of our own behavior and encourages us to conduct ourselves in an appropriate way.

Advice for our sons:

For our young brothers, we love you, and we only want the best for you. We have a few words of advice for you:

1. Watch the company you keep and the so-called friends that you surround yourself with. Do not keep hanging around people who show no regard or curiosity for your faith. Never forget you are Muslim.

2. The Prophet Muhammad (PBUH) said that when you finish one task, one project, or one goal, immediately begin another one. Don't allow yourself to become stagnant or inactive.

3. Keep busy with positive people and projects. There is an old saying: "Idle hands and idle minds are the devil's workshop." So don't be idle.

4. Whatever field or endeavor you are in or choose to go in, be it business, medicine, law, or if you are working for someone, always remember to put your best effort into whatever the job is.

5. Allah says in the Holy Qur'an to "revere the wombs that bore you." And Prophet Muhammad (PBUH) tells us that our mothers hold higher esteem than our fathers. Although you are to respect you parents, your mother has a special place according to Allah and Prophet Muhammad. In life, we come from various wombs. First, our mothers, next, our communities, third, our chosen field of endeavor. All of those environments shape and mold us into what we are and what we are to become, so never underestimate the value of their influence.

A man-up proposal
Solution

A life skills development seminar (mining our own business)

Purpose:

Create a program where we teach our young people the principles and values of life and business skills such as:

- how to carry themselves in public
- the importance of good manners

- the benefits of always having a respectful attitude
- the value of being a life-long student, not intimidated about learning new skills
- how to pursue business interests, research, and etc.
- the importance of good diction
- the difference between failure and success
- the need to prioritize time and resources
- being organized and clean

Men and boys gathering
Some comments and solutions

Greetings, may the peace and blessings of G-D be upon you. Young men, there is a responsibility to the community, society, and world that is left in your charge or care. We all will inherit responsibility. Everybody has it, but whether he or she will accept it or not is another thing. The Creator said in scripture that He created the world for the benefit of mankind to discover its vast resources in the air and earth, to study the creatures, plants, and climates; to learn more sophisticated ways of traveling, such as studying how birds fly. And we were blessed with airplanes. We have studied how the fish lives and swims. Now, we have boats, ships, and submarines.

In addition, man was taught to harvest and mine the resources of the earth for his benefit. G-D taught man to also plow the earth for its minerals, plants, and study the food and medicine that is derived from these sources. Therefore, man has been given much direction in scripture. Now, all man has to do is respect and use the total package, for he will be much better off. The scripture says that G-D created mankind into different nations and tribes so that man would get to know one another and not despise or hate or be jealous of each other.

G-D created us unique with our own personality. Our very fingertips are different on each individual. Everybody has his or her own identity, but we also have that common identity which is human.

Always remember that Abraham (PBUH) is the father of all three faiths. And remember the wise advice that Luqman gave to his son:

> O my dear son! Never associate anything with G-D in worship, for associating others with Him is truly the worst of all wrongs. He adds, O my dear son! Even if a deed were the weight of a mustard seed— be it hidden in a rock or in the heavens or the earth—G-D will bring it forth. Surely, G-D is Most Subtle, All Aware. And do not turn your nose up to people, nor walk pridefully upon the earth. Surely, G-D does not like whoever is arrogant, boastful. Be moderate in your pace. And lower your voice, for the ugliest of all voices is certainly the braying of donkeys. (Holy Qur'an 31:13–19)

In his advice, Luqman reminds his son of the oneness of Allah and against committing shirk. He points out that

Allah knows all and will hold us responsible for all of our deeds, good and bad. And he exhorts his son to be modest in his relationships and demeanor. This is good advice for fathers, sons, and brothers who have faith.

Remembrance of G-D is the greatest saving force, and our leader Imam W. Deen Mohammed (RAA) has called us to "remake the work" by building the model community that Prophet Moses sought and Prophet Muhammad established in Medina. That is the role or responsibility of Muslim men—fathers, sons, and brothers, to follow the example of the prophets and build the *ummah* or a community under G-D's governance. Amen.

"Respect Ye One Another."

CHAPTER 8

Brotherhood of Man

Thank G-D for the Abrahamic faiths. Judaism is the monotheistic religion of the Jews developed among the ancient Hebrews. Judaism does not focus on abstract cosmological concepts. Judaism focuses on the relationship between G-D and man. It also focuses on the relationship between human beings. If there is a dispute or conflict between which law should apply in a given situation (Torah or Rabbi's Law), the Torah takes precedence.

Christianity espouses that there is only one G-D whom they call Father as taught by Jesus Christ (PBUH). Jesus was sent to save mankind from death and sin. He taught his adherents to love G-D and their neighbors, believe in a Creator who is all-powerful, and believe in baptism. Jesus said he came to fulfill the law of Moses, and that there is life after death. Christians believe that through the spiritual realm, they get a taste of the afterlife here on Earth.

Al-Islam is the religion of Muslims. Muslim means one who surrenders to the will of G-D. To become a Muslim requires a declaration of faith or as we call it, "Taking the shahada by saying, 'There is no G-D but G-D, and Muhammad is the Messenger of G-D.'"

Al-Islam, the religion of peace and submission, teaches the importance of both belief and practice wherein one is insufficient without the other. It teaches belief in one G-D, the Creator of the heavens and earth. Muslims believe in angels that carry out G-D's orders throughout the universe, and in all the revealed books of G-D and all of His prophets, which include Adam, Abraham, Noah, Moses, Jesus, David, Solomon, and Muhammad (May G-D's Peace be upon them). Muslims also believe in the day of judgement and divine decree.

How are these faiths similar? They all believe that Abraham is the father of all three faiths (Abrahamic faiths). Just what do they have in common? They all believe in one Creator as monotheistic faiths. Their followers are required to obey religious laws and revelations that came to them from G-D before their time, during their time, and after their time. The Abrahamic faiths believe that actions are as equally important as belief and that G-D exists and He is one and all-powerful and eternal. Additionally, prayer is to be directed to G-D alone, for no intermediary is necessary. The words of all the prophets are true; the Torah is the first five books of the Bible, G-D will reward the good and punish the wicked, and they have the belief in the resurrection of the dead on the day of judgment.

The Abrahamic faiths are the continuous message from the Creator as guidance for mankind. Because of the evolutionary nature of Judaism, Christianity, and Islam, Muslims believe that G-D is one, humanity is one, and religion is one.

Reconstruction
A new life for a new people

Have you heard yet—freedom—well, act like it! Juneteenth 1865 is the beginning of a new life for a new people. Juneteenth is known as Independence Day or Freedom Day. It is an American holiday that commemorates the June 19, 1865, announcement of emancipation of slaves in the state of Texas. More generally speaking, the emancipation of enslaved blacks throughout the former confederacy of the southern United States. Its name is a portmanteau or combination of the words June and the nineteenth, the date of its celebration. June nineteenth is recognized as a special day of observance in all fifty states.

What we must recognize is that the Emancipation Proclamation, signed into law, January 1, 1863, was a step toward abolishing slavery. For it only addressed the freeing of slaves in the states that were in open rebellion against the unity of the United States of America. Those states were known as the Confederacy and included: Arkansas, Texas, Louisiana, except for certain counties, Mississippi, Alabama, Florida, Georgia, South Carolina, North Carolina, Virginia, except West Virginia. However, slavery in states that were not in rebellion against the United States of America was not abolished. The Emancipation Proclamation encouraged slaves under the control of the Confederacy to run away to Union and held positions where they were employed to help the Union cause. It acknowledged that these freed slaves could join in the fight as soldiers, and that the war had finally become a war to abolish slavery.

The Civil War began April 12, 1861, and ended May 9, 1865. Based upon the Juneteenth date, enslaved Africans heard news of their freedom in Texas, more than a month after the Civil War had ended and two years and six months after the Emancipation Proclamation. Additionally, slavery was abolished throughout the United States of America upon ratification of the Thirteenth Amendment to the Constitution on December 6, 1865. The Thirteenth Amendment reads:

Section 1

Neither slavery nor involuntary servitude, except as a punishment for crime whereof the party shall have been duly convicted, shall exist within the United States, or any place subject to their jurisdiction.

Section 2

Congress shall have power to enforce this article by appropriate legislation.

The Thirteenth Amendment physically freed African Americans from the bondage of slavery, yet the exception of slavery as punishment for a crime was a loophole used by many southern states through Jim Crow laws to re-enslave many of our ancestors, whether guilty or not.

The Fourteenth Amendment granted citizenship to the former slaves and equal protection under the law. It also provided guidance in eliminating members of Congress on the state and federal levels or executive or judicial officers who are insurrectionists or in rebellion against the Constitution of the United States of America. As well as disenfranchising individual citizens who participated in an insurrection or rebellion against the Constitution of the United States of America. January 6, 2021, was a day when American citizens once again rebelled against the United States of America. It is a date that will live in infamy and has not been fully addressed according to the guidelines of the Fourteenth Amendment to the United States Constitution:

Section 1.

All persons born or naturalized in the United States, and subject to the jurisdiction thereof, are citizens of the United States and of the state wherein they reside. No state shall make or enforce any law which shall abridge the privileges or immunities of citizens of the United States; nor shall any state deprive any person of life, liberty, or property, without due process of law; nor deny to any person within its jurisdiction the equal protection of the laws.

Section 2.

Representatives shall be apportioned among the several states according to their respective numbers, counting the whole number of persons in each state, excluding Indians not taxed. But when the right to vote at any election for the choice of electors for President and Vice President of the United States, Representatives in Congress, the executive and judicial officers of a state, or the members of the legislature thereof, is denied to any of the male inhabitants of such state, being twenty-one years of age, and citizens of the United States, or in any way abridged, except for participation in rebellion, or other crime, the basis of representation therein shall be reduced in the proportion which the number of such male citizens shall bear to the whole number of male citizens twenty-one years of age in such state.

Section 3.

No person shall be a Senator or Representative in Congress, or elector of President and Vice President, or hold any office, civil or military, under the United States, or under any state, who, having previously taken an oath, as a member of Congress, or as an officer of the United States, or as a member of any state legislature, or as an executive or judicial officer of any state, to support the Constitution of the United States, shall have engaged in insurrection or rebellion against the same, or given aid or comfort to the enemies thereof. But Congress may by a vote of two-thirds of each House, remove such disability.

Section 4.

The validity of the public debt of the United States, authorized by law, including debts incurred for payment of pensions and bounties for services in suppressing insurrection or rebellion, shall not be questioned. But neither the United States nor any state shall assume or pay any debt or obligation incurred in aid of insurrection or rebellion against the United States, or any claim for the loss or emancipation of any slave; but all such debts, obligations and claims shall be held illegal and void.

Section 5.

The Congress shall have power to enforce, by appropriate legislation, the provisions of this article.

The Fifteenth Amendment to the US Constitution gave African American men, who were former slaves, the right to vote:

Section 1.

The right of citizens of the United States to vote shall not be denied or abridged by the United States or by any state on account of race, color, or previous condition of servitude.

Section 2.

The Congress shall have power to enforce this article by appropriate legislation.

Yes, we are a new people. We are 156 years out of slavery and fifty-three years from the end of Jim Crow and segregation, so we have a lot of catching up to do in social development. However, we, as a new people, must realize that we cannot follow in the footsteps of our former oppressors, for we will become a caricature of them. As all people have done, we must throw our lot into the hands of G-D and seek our divine destiny so that G-D may forge a new man and a new woman. And with His help, we can make a better world in which we not only free ourselves but also all of humanity. Imam W. Deen Mohammed (RAA) has challenged us to make the world and society a better place by providing an alternative model of community life.

Peace

Dear people, our current condition in our community is at a critical point. It seems that love, respect, and concern for one another is at an all-time low in the history of our community. We have some very serious moral and ethical problems in our hearts and minds (in our soul). If we don't address them and get back to a lifestyle of respecting age-old principles, the Creator will dismiss us from this existence.

Dear brothers and sisters, a lot of our young people are following in the footsteps of a mindset that doesn't have our best interests at heart. We need to improve our moral and economic position in our society. As mentioned earlier, our children tend to follow what is popular and current in our society. But we know that values that are popular and current can serve as a people's demise or destruction. So if we have moral issues in ourselves and in our neighborhood and we are not addressing them, then those results will be ours to deal with. Let's make the right decision—let's face reality.

A viable or relatively functioning family and community usually pass strong values and practices onto the next generations, no matter what the popular trends are. As a people, we have not been successful at doing that consistently (study the period from slavery, reconstruction to the present). Consequently, our young people are misbehaving and going wild out here. With no sense of direction and responsibility as it regards the future direction of our people and our community, it seems we have no picture of how we want our lives to look like twenty, thirty, or fifty years from now.

Our community life has declined dramatically because of moral failures, so we, once again, need to teach strong, lasting values and morality in our schools but especially in our sacred places of worship (homes, churches, masjids, and etc.). If we don't change our current behavior, our future will be a very dark place. But we can reattach ourselves to a principled life by showing respect for high values and developing a genuine love, respect, and concern for one another in our families and communities. This may seem, to some, as a small issue, but people that lose moral footing risk losing their identity as a civilized community. And people, we have come really close to losing our moral footing. We can get our balance back! But we have to exercise moral and historical courage.

We need to take from our past all that was valuable and good. And after analyzing our history, we will leave those things that no longer serve our purpose. We must salvage what we can from this generation and give a lot of focused attention and resources to our "little ones."

Imam W. Deen Mohammed in a lecture titled "America's Dilemma Faith and Corruption," says:

> Muslims are a people who have been raised not just for Muslims alone. Allah says in His Qur'an that you are the best community raised up for humankind. You have an obligation to yourself, your family, your neighborhood, your Muslim community, as well as to non-Muslims living near you or at a distance to promote good. That obligation goes throughout the whole humanity.

In conclusion, we must, once again, make family life, marriage, and morality the most important institutions in our community. We are all in this together. Like Dr. King said, "Either we will live together as a civilized community or die together as fools"—you choose.

To the citizens of the United States

I thank the Creator for this opportunity to address you briefly on a subject that is dear to me, which is respect for the human individual. I'd like to share an observation with you or advocate for an idea whose time has come. I don't know if we all have noticed, but our children are growing up in an interesting new world. One in which humans from all parts of the world and from all cultural backgrounds are finally beginning to realize the benefits and blessings of the whole human family, by becoming more familiar with one another. Therefore, how can we all contribute to this universal human family?

You know that we all harbor a lot of misperceptions about one another because of a lack of knowledge, incorrect knowledge, narrow-minded arrogance, or just a lack of appreciation for humans that may be culturally different from ourselves. But I know that we need a broader, more inclusive attitude and vision for our community as we go forward. A vision that teaches us and our children how to treat and care about our fellow human beings better for the overall benefit and survival of our society, as we know it. This vision includes sincerely sharing our world's limited resources in a more equitable fashion. You can call our current behavior what you want, but Grandma called it greed and selfishness.

If we don't adopt this new type of mentality, we will experience a society that will become increasingly more mistrusting and volatile. However, our children deserve better, and we can honor what they deserve if we act now and stop being selfish. After all, you can't take all the money and material that you have accumulated with you. Although, some people act like they can but they can't. Try it!

So let us do all we can as good citizens and public servants and start to address the root causes of crime, unemployment, moral issues, and low self-esteem among our people. And we must create more opportunities in our communities and neighborhoods through the creation of more jobs, better economic situations, and higher ethical standards. We cannot keep pushing the problems to the next generation or down the street. Let's solve them.

Some of our young people need real rehabilitation, not situations where they get into trouble and keep returning to the same environment. And the same bad things are waiting for them there, so we, the individual, family, and the community experience recidivism. We want them to have real opportunities for success, but what have we done to prepare an environment or community that is conducive to human success?

The Honorable Elijah Muhammad (RAA) is reported to have said that builders are respected, and beggars are rejected, which he considered to be a universal statement. Therefore, African Americans cannot expect the respect of other people until we begin to build community life for the benefit of ourselves and to benefit the rest of humanity. Imam W. Deen Muhammad confirms that point when he says:

> African Americans don't have the courage
> to establish their ethnicity like the Irish, the
> Italians and others, including the recent

immigrants who are now coming into this country from Asia, Cuba and elsewhere. African Americans don't have the courage to let the white man know that they have a concern for their own kind and are not depending on him to direct that concern. They are afraid to talk like a man within the hearing range of the white man, even though they know that they would be doing nothing but accepting the responsibility that would bring them into the admiration of the American people.

I say to the Muslims, let us be more responsible for ourselves, our family members, our neighborhoods, our personal property and our people. Let us show America that we are not of the common run; we are special people with our own sense of direction, and our own sense of responsibility. And believe me, if we do this, we will go forward and become leaders of our own destiny in America overnight. (Students of W. D. Mohammed, "Hagar's Children")

True freedom demands that we take more responsibility for our own lives, our own destiny, our own view of ourselves, and our own aspirations as Americans.

"Develop Courage"

CHAPTER 9

Solutions

Freedom metaphors and talking points

Over seven billion people share this planet, and there are over 265 different dialects and many cultural groups.

The challenge

How do we share these limited resources and learn to benefit from our perceived differences and recognize the common qualities we have as human beings?

Our human identity is our best identity, not our color or culture. One sacred trait that we have in common, as members of this human species, is our innate ability to have genuine concern for our inherent human excellence and other human beings. Other unique qualities that we share among ourselves are our intelligence, our ability to plan our lives for future generations, and our ability to plan on a high cognitive level.

Our good old people always told us, but we didn't always listen, "to watch the people you hang around." Don't get caught up in their "mess," for they will bring you down or get you into trouble.

Your cultural identity is an African American to the degree that you are committed to and connected to your history and legacy.

It is possible to lose your identity, who you are.

As humans, we are creatures of influence. Our environment has a lot to do with our disposition and ultimate development—nature versus nurture should be recognized as nature and nurture working together. We should always strive to be in touch with our nature as human beings— civilized beings.

What were all our efforts for? But to bring us to a "better" place.

Bibliography

1976–1978

Bari attended San Jose City College and, at that time, was the Black Student Union (BSU) president. Bari also attended Howard University from 1978 to 1981 and served as the Muslim student coordinator for an organization called Muslim Students for Universal Peace. Bari earned his bachelor's degree from the University of Maryland.

1996–2008

Bari Muhammed has been in the community of believers under the leadership of Imam W. Deen Mohammed since 1975. He has been a strong and consistent supporter from the beginning. And in 1996, he became one of the close aides to Imam Mohammed. He worked with and assisted our leader with community development initiatives.

During this association, he was instrumental in developing the engine that sustained the community. For example, he worked with promoting W. D. Mohammed Publications, the collective purchasing program, the business suit initiative, halal meat productions, health products purchase and distribution, and etc. He traveled extensively while supporting these programs around the US and to Jamaica, sourcing products that our community could use. Bari Muhammed and Imam Abu Qadir El-Amin were the first individuals chosen to explore business opportunities in China for the Muslim community under the leadership of Imam Mohammed.

Bari has raised two sons as a single parent and is considering getting married again. He worked as a counselor with a youth program in Washington, DC, with young men from broken homes. He also served as an advisory neighborhood commissioner in Southeast Washington, DC.

1996–2008

Bari started the Father & Son's Breakfast at our annual National Convention, encouraging fathers and sons to have stronger relationships. After the physical passing of our leader, Bari Muhammed moved to Greenville, North Carolina (the place of his birth), to work in community relations. He was on the community relations committee and worked with the mayor, city council, and police chief to make the community a better place.

2008–2017

Bari served as a liaison between the community of Greenville and the city council. While living in Greenville, North Carolina, he worked with middle school students in the science, technology, engineering, math (STEM) program. After working there about three years, he decided to move to Charlotte, North Carolina. Bari taught fourth graders under President Obama's After School Enrichment program, a charter school. He has earned an associate of arts and a bachelor of arts degree in management studies. After moving to Atlanta, he began working with youth at Ridgeview Institute.

2017–Present

Bari Muhammed currently resides in Charlotte, North Carolina. He said that it has been challenging living in new places without the traditional support networks, but he thanks G-D for the experiences. Bari loves business, physical fitness, healthy eating, and family life.

BARI MUHAMMED

"Exercising Our Freedom to Remake Our World"

COMMENTS

Growing up, I had the opportunity to watch my father's heavy involvement in our Islamic community at both local and national levels. I also had the unique experience of living with a mostly single father. These experiences were formative for me in my youth. As an adult with a family of my own, the challenge and importance of balancing home and community has been brought more clearly into focus.

Some of my earliest memories were at the masjid. If something was going on at the masjid, we were often there. I didn't know it at the time, but the continuity of our community relied on the entire family having a connection to the masjid. It didn't stop there; we also attended and were involved with the community's national convention. I've met lifelong friends there and even met my wife there. My father was directly involved in the community's business initiatives. That was very important to the spirit of the community. We have a history of emphasizing self-reliance. Coming together to do business whether at a large or small scale makes the difference between that emphasis being reality or just rhetoric.

That self-reliance translated to our home life as well. From cooking and cleaning to painting fences and minor repair work, from a young age, we learned what it took to maintain a home. I came to notice that living with a single father was unique among my friends and classmates. It seems there is a common thread with taking a hands-on approach to one's family and being proactive in your community.

Ultimately *Community Life*, as described by Imam W. D. Mohammed, was a guiding principle for my father. It connected how he approached our home, our masjid, and our larger community. That approach continues with my family as well.

—Omar Muhammad

Bari takes us back to how it all began for so many of us, that sense and importance of community. He reminds us of the values, the positive examples, the leadership, and the resiliency to strive for something better, reminding us that we stand on the shoulders of our community. Regardless of our varied cultures, the life lessons, and the knowledge we gain from our community, it all becomes a part of our history. Well done, my friend!

—Donna "D" Artist

This book is written by a man who worked and walked with Imam W. Deen Mohammed during his leadership. This book is a must-read for anyone who wants to understand community life.

—E. Na'eem Syed

"THINK AGAIN—HAVE VISION"

Advice from Imam W. D. Mohammed

Imam W. D. Mohammed said to me, "Brother Bari, I like your writing, your articles." He said, "I look forward to your article and that your articles are the first ones I go to, when I pick up the paper [MJ]. Keep on writing."

The imam (WDM) told me that most of us aren't ready yet for what we have been given; what his leadership is offering (freedom, community life, clarity in religion, and the community-building initiatives that were presented to us). He said, "Enough of us are ready, but go slow and be patient."

OUR LOVE

A Community's Dilemma
(Our World Minus Spirituality and Common
Sense—Getting Back on the Straight Path)

Our love is like a plant out of water; slowly dying like that
plant, our love has withered and turned to dust, like our
separation, a must.

> Getting or staying away from those things
> that bring us down as individuals and as a
> cultural group (African Americans).

> (*A must needs do so.*)

Our love is like a plant out of water; slowly dying like
that plant, our love has withered and turned to dust, like
our separation, a must.

> The first step in solving a problem is to
> admit that there is a problem—then move
> toward a solution.

> (*A must needs do so.*)

Our love is like a plant out of water; slowly dying like that plant, our love has withered and turned to dust, like our separation, a must.

> Give up those things that you like that you know are destroying you: bad eating habits, knowing the truth but keep believing the lies, keeping bad company, etc.

(A must needs do so.)

Our love is like a plant out of water; slowly dying like that plant, our love has withered and turned to dust, like our separation, a must.

> Live, think, and do what's right or perish.
> Love G-D, build character and love thyself, the human being, especially your own cultural group.

(A must needs do so.)

Our love is like a plant out of water; slowly dying like that plant, our love has withered and turned to dust, like our separation, a must.

> Do the best you can until you know better—then when you know better, do better. (Maya Angelou)

(A must needs do so.)

Our love is like a plant out of water; slowly dying like that plant, our love has withered and turned to dust, like our separation, a must.

> May we think of freedom, not as the right
> to do as we please, but as the opportunity
> to do what is right. (Peter Marshall)

> (*A must needs do so.*)

Our love is like a plant out of water; slowly dying like that plant, our love has withered and turned to dust, like our separation, a must.

> Getting further away from bad people
> and bad ideas as that one can grow into a
> whole person—it is easier to build strong
> children than to repair broken men.
> (Frederick Douglas)

> (*A must needs do so.*)

Our love is like a plant out of water; slowly dying like that plant, our love has withered and turned to dust, like our separation, a must.

> Real mind moves from a state of weakness
> to a state of strength so the world will not
> be destroyed by those who do evil, but

by those who watch them without doing anything. (Albert Einstein)

(*A must needs do so.*)

Our love is like a plant out of water; slowly dying like that plant, our love has withered and turned to dust, like our separation, a must.

> A-LA. A degraded lifestyle that serves only Satan and an arrogant attitude that's not worthy of consideration in a righteous world.

(*A must needs do so.*)

Our love is like a plant out of water; slowly dying like that plant, our love has withered and turned to dust, like our separation, a must.

> From wrong ideas and no morals—from the lies, the deceit, and ignorance of false history and ignoring the importance of not burdening our children with these narrow-minded perceptions of civilization that we were exposed to in our youth— *never again.*

(*A must needs do so.*)

Our love is like a plant out of water; slowly dying like that plant, our love has withered and turned to dust, like our separation, a must.

> Separate—move away from a lack of faith, love, lack of character, consideration for others' feelings, lack of rational thinking and concerns.

> (*A must needs do so.*)

Our love is like a plant out of water; slowly dying like that plant, our love has withered and turned to dust, like our separation, a must.

> The sure reality—like life and death and that continuous cycle of obedience, willingly or unwillingly characterizes everything in the universe—no escape.

> (*A must needs do so.*)

Our love is like a plant out of water; slowly dying like that plant, our love has withered and turned to dust, like our separation, a must.

> *From* ignorance and lack of commitment—forever pushing that "Sisyphus Rock" up the hill just to have it roll back down when you are almost at the top—

again and again because of a lack of prepa-
ration and planning or the right type of
help.

(*A must needs do so.*)

Our love is like a plant out of water; slowly dying like
that plant, our love has withered and turned to dust, like
our separation, a must.

Stay away from "greed"; get all you can,
can all you get, and sit on the can; share
the wealth and the love. (Naim Akbar)

(*A must needs do so.*)

Our love is like a plant out of water; slowly dying like
that plant, our love has withered and turned to dust, like
our separation, a must.

ABOUT THE AUTHOR

Bari Muhammed is the author of this literary work entitled *Community Life*. This work was inspired by his work and association with a great man, the leader of the largest Muslim community in the Western Hemisphere (USA) Imam W. Deen Mohammed. The *Imam* passed on September 9, 2008, but the efforts to establish community life continues. Some of the work he did with his community was as a community liaison, assisting in organizing conventions, setting up speaking engagements for the leader, and working on developing business initiatives and traveling to assist with events. He was a single father of two great boys for a while. He went to San Jose City College in California to Howard University, and he graduated from the University of Maryland.